# Feed My Sheep

## LEADERSHIP IDEAS FOR LATTER-DAY SHEPHERDS

Alexander B. Morrison

Deseret Book Company
Salt Lake City, Utah

**Library of Congress Cataloging-in-Publication Data**

Morrison, Alexander B.
    Feed my sheep / by Alexander B. Morrison.
       p.  cm.
    Includes index.
    ISBN 0-87579-605-2
    1. Leadership—Religious aspects—Christianity.  2. Pastoral theology—Mormon Church.  3. Church of Jesus Christ of Latter-day Saints—Membership.  4. Mormon Church—Membership. I. Title.
BX8643.L4M67   1992
253—dc20                             92-25690
                                                  CIP

Printed in the United States of America

10   9   8   7   6   5   4   3   2   1

# Contents

# *Preface*

This book is not an official publication of The Church of Jesus Christ of Latter-day Saints. No one asked me to write it. The views and ideas presented herein are my own and do not necessarily represent the position or view of the Church. Similarly, I am also fully responsible for errors and omissions in the text. All royalties received from sales of the book have been assigned to the Church Educational System for African scholarship activities.

This book is dedicated to my wife, Shirley, one of the great shepherdesses of the kingdom. Her example of selfless love and service inspires and humbles me.

I owe a special debt of gratitude to Carolyn Hyde for her great skill in typing and proofreading the manuscript. Her suggestions for improvement were invariably correct.

# Introduction

Many years of labor in the fields of the Lord have impressed upon me the importance of the shepherd's task. Leaders have always played an indispensable role in the work of the kingdom. They are the Lord's undershepherds, entrusted with the care of His flock, accountable for the salvation of those in their charge.

The scriptures solemnly certify that God will hold accountable shepherds who abandon the sheep in their charge; who fail to magnify their calling, whatever it is; who act like hirelings rather than stewards of a sacred trust. These sober words of the Nephite prophet Jacob drive home the point: "And we [Jacob and his brother Joseph] did magnify our office unto the Lord, taking upon us the responsibility, answering the sins of the people upon our own heads if we did not teach them the word of God with all diligence; wherefore, by laboring with our might their blood might not come upon our garments; otherwise their blood would come upon our garments, and we would not be found spotless at the last day." (Jacob 1:19.)

Jacob's somber reminder of the responsibility shepherds bear reiterates a recurring scriptural theme: God's righteous anger is directed against shepherds who do not feed the flock. Throughout the ages, His prophets have spoken often of God's indignation toward such miscreant servants. Said the Lord to Ezekiel:

My sheep wandered through all the mountains, and upon every high hill: yea, my flock was scattered upon all the face of the earth, and none did search or seek after them. Therefore, ye shepherds, hear the word of the Lord; as I live, saith the Lord God, surely because my flock became a prey, and my flock became meat to every beast of the field, because there was no shepherd, neither did my shepherds search for my flock, but the shepherds fed themselves, and fed not my flock; therefore, O ye shepherds, hear the word of the Lord; Thus saith the Lord God; Behold, I am against the shepherds; and I will require my flock at their hand, and cause them to cease from feeding the flock; neither shall the shepherds feed themselves any more; for I will deliver my flock from their mouth, that they may not be meat for them. (Ezekiel 34:6–10.)

Jeremiah lamented, "My people hath been lost sheep: their shepherds have caused them to go astray, they have turned them away on the mountains: they have gone from mountain to hill, they have forgotten their restingplace." (Jeremiah 50:6.) Jesus dismissed delinquent shepherds as "blind leaders of the blind." (Matthew 15:14.) The message is clear: shepherds are expected to do all that they can to move the work of the Lord forward, "every man stand[ing] in his own office, and labor[ing] in his own calling." (D&C 84:109.)

Many, perhaps most, who are called to the shepherd's task feel unprepared, inadequate, ill-trained — lacking the wisdom, understanding, and skill required of the Lord's servants. Theirs is the humility of the Prophet Amos who declared, "I was no prophet, neither was I a prophet's son; but I was an herdman, and a gatherer of sycomore fruit: And the Lord took me as I followed the flock, and the Lord said unto me, Go." (Amos 7:14–15.)

Notwithstanding their weaknesses and inadequacies, however, the Lord calls his shepherds to their task, seeing in them divine possibilities for growth and service. This book is written in an attempt to help shepherds better understand their responsibilities. It is not a "how-to-do-it" book on leadership techniques; such can be found in nearly every book shop in the land. Others are better qualified than I to judge the merits of such publications. For myself, I have little confidence in "quick fixes" that promise instant success with little effort.

Nor is this publication intended as a definitive treatise on secular leadership as practiced in the world. The management literature is full of articles dealing with various aspects of this immensely complex field, and numerous scholars have written extensively about it. My intention is more humble: I desire to provide the Lord's undershepherds with some principles to guide them in their task, that they might be good and faithful servants.

# CHAPTER ONE

# The Essence of Leadership

The public has always been fascinated by strong, successful leaders, both in war and in peace. Numerous attempts have been made over the centuries to describe the personality traits of great leaders or the patterns of behavior that distinguish leader from follower. Why are some people leaders and others followers? What is it that distinguishes a George Washington, a Winston Churchill, or a Joseph Smith from others? What is the source of the power of great leaders? Can leadership be learned, or is it an innate trait brought from elsewhere? Is there some way to predict who the leaders of tomorrow will be? These and related questions about leaders have tantalized for centuries. The answers to them are important if we are to learn how to lead "in the Lord's way," as faithful undershepherds.

Some may say blithely that it's not all that hard to describe a great leader. Misguided male chauvinists may proclaim that a great leader must be a man. While many great leaders have indeed been men, what about Florence Nightingale, Joan of Arc, or Elizabeth I? Another might believe that great leaders are majestic of stature, standing out from the crowd on the basis of size and physical attainments alone. They forget that Napoleon, Admiral Nelson, and Spencer W. Kimball were small of stature, as have been many other superb leaders. A third misguided soul might proclaim that great leaders must be extraordinary orators, capable of inspiring hearts and spirits by the power of their voice. But Moses, one of the greatest leaders of all time, by his own admission was slow and hesitant of speech. (See Exodus 4:10.) For every example that can be given of a leader possessing one characteristic or another, a second example can be found of an equally great leader who didn't exhibit the attribute in question in any remarkable way at all! Leadership is much more than a collection of attributes. We must look elsewhere for its definition.

## Situational Leadership

Most experts now agree, at least in general terms, that leadership does not depend primarily on personality; rather, it is situational. In other words, leadership effectiveness depends upon the relationship in a particular situation between the personality of the leader, the task to be accomplished, and the attitudes and perceptions of both leader and followers. What is effective leadership in one situation just won't work in another. "Stonewall" Jackson was a superb wartime leader, but I doubt he would have excelled as president of the local PTA!

Some situations—emergencies, for example—call for a task-oriented approach to leadership, with clearly defined lines of authority and instruction. Orders are given by whoever is in charge, and those who receive them are expected to follow those orders without question. This leadership style works best when there just isn't time for extensive explanation, discussion, and shared goal-setting; when following instructions exactly is essential for success; and when the effects of failure to take the correct action are substantial. If the chapel is on fire, it's not appropriate to hold a ward council to decide whether to evacuate the building!

2

Some leaders (and some followers, too) function best under these command-and-obey circumstances. Others, however, are uncomfortable and don't function well in such highly structured, rigid situations. Furthermore, most problems simply do not require a military-command style of leadership for their effective solution. Whenever possible, wise leaders involve those affected by the decisions they make by explaining, asking for advice, and enlisting support and commitment rather than requiring mere acquiescence. They seek informed commitment rather than blind obedience.

Wise leaders thus are flexible in adapting to differences between subordinates. The style and substance of their leadership varies, depending on the nature of the problem to be solved and the people available to solve it. They keep their eyes and thoughts firmly on the goal they seek to accomplish but are flexible on the choice of methods used. They learn to match people and situations. They learn to "read" people, some of whom do best if given only general guidelines and allowed to "run with the ball," while others require more detailed instruction and coaching. Some prefer routine; others thrive on challenge. Leaders must, then, become applied psychologists in matching individuals and circumstances to obtain desired results.

This axiom is well illustrated by an episode in the life of Captain James Cook, the intrepid Scot who was one of the great seafarers of all time. Possessed of restless energy, unusual organizing ability, and dogged persistence in the face of what to others were insurmountable difficulties, Cook discovered the Great Barrier Reef off the northeast coast of Australia, charted the coasts of New Zealand and Tonga, and circumnavigated the globe at the southernmost latitude (proving that a long-postulated great Southern Continent did not, in fact, exist).

Although Cook is honored in our day because of his

great voyages of discovery, in his own time he was recognized because of what he did to improve the health and save the lives of sailors. On long sea voyages scurvy was a curse that decimated the majority of crews, whose diet was composed almost entirely of rancid salt pork and weevilly sea biscuit. When Vasco da Gama, the great Portuguese navigator, made the first voyage by a European around the southern tip of Africa and across the Indian Ocean to India in 1498, he is said to have lost 100 of his 170 men from the dread disease with its symptoms of bleeding, swollen joints, loosened teeth, anemia, and lassitude. James Lind, a Scottish naval surgeon, demonstrated in 1753 that citrus fruit would prevent and even cure the disease. (The practice of giving lime juice to sailors of the Royal Navy gave rise in later years to use of the term *limey* to describe the English in general.)

Cook, who evidently was not aware of Lind's work, nevertheless had heard of the value of fruit in preventing scurvy. He experimented with various fruits, grasses, and vegetables as scurvy preventatives. So successful was he that in two long sea voyages, each lasting two to three years, Cook seems not to have lost a single sailor from scurvy.

In his experimenting, Cook found that sauerkraut would prevent scurvy. But there was a problem. His sailors, traditionally suspicious of new-fangled ideas and intensely conservative in their habits, refused to eat the stuff. Cook solved the problem by being flexible in what he did but persistent in what he aimed to accomplish. In his journal he recorded this great lesson in leadership:

> The Sour Krout the Men at first would not eate untill I put in practice a Method I never once knew to fail with seamen, and this was to have some of it dress'd every Day for the Cabbin Table, and permitted all the Officers without exception to make

use of it and left it to the option of the Men either to take as much as they pleased or none at all; but this practice was not continued above a week before I found it necessary to put every one on board to an Allowance, for such are the Tempers and disposissions of Seamen in general that whatever you give them out of the Common way, altho it be ever so much for their good yet it will not go down with them and you will hear nothing but murmurings gainest the man that first invented it; but the Moment they see their Superiors set a Value upon it, it becomes the finest stuff in the World and the inventer [an] . . . honest fellow. (Daniel J. Boorstin, *The Discoverers* [New York: Vintage Books, 1983], p. 289.)

How does one reconcile the notion that leaders are the product of situations with the scriptural evidence that God chose His rulers "before the world was"? Recall these words from Abraham 3:22–23: "The Lord had shown unto me, Abraham, the intelligences that were organized before the world was; and among all these there were many of the noble and great ones; and God saw these souls that they were good, and he stood in the midst of them, and he said: These I will make my rulers . . . and he said unto me: Abraham, thou art one of them; thou wast chosen before thou wast born."

In considering the applicability of these words to leadership in general, it is wise to keep in mind that God is talking about *His* leaders, not those of the world, whose motives, aspirations, and methods may or may not be worthy of divine approbation. Also, even those chosen for the Lord's work "before the world was" must prove themselves worthy to receive anticipated blessings. They are foreordained, not predestined, for greatness. If they do not prove faithful, they will be removed and another will take their place. After the loss of 116 pages of manuscript

5

translated from the "Book of Lehi," Joseph Smith was chastised by his loving Lord:

> Remember, remember that it is not the work of God that is frustrated, but the work of men; For although a man may have many revelations, and have power to do many mighty works, yet if he boasts in his own strength, and sets at naught the counsels of God, and follows after the dictates of his own will and carnal desires, he must fall and incur the vengeance of a just God upon him.
>
> Behold, you have been entrusted with these things, but how strict were your commandments; and remember also the promises which were made to you, if you did not transgress them.
>
> And behold, how oft you have transgressed the commandments and the laws of God, and have gone on in the persuasions of men.
>
> For, behold, you should not have feared man more than God. Although men set at naught the counsels of God, and despise his words —
>
> Yet you should have been faithful; and he would have extended his arm and supported you against all the fiery darts of the adversary; and he would have been with you in every time of trouble.
>
> Behold, thou art Joseph, and thou wast chosen to do the work of the Lord, but because of transgression, if thou art not aware thou wilt fall.
>
> But remember, God is merciful; therefore, repent of that which thou hast done which is contrary to the commandment which I gave you, and thou art still chosen, and art again called to the work;
>
> Except thou do this, thou shalt be delivered up and become as other men, and have no more gift. (D&C 3:3–11.)

In other words, God chooses His leaders, but they may disqualify themselves if they select the wrong paths. They are, of course, free to do so; but they must pay whatever price is involved, up to and including forfeiture of their status as one of the Lord's undershepherds.

I believe there is nothing inherently antagonistic between the views that leadership is situational and that God chooses His leaders. Perhaps His role is to ensure that those whom He has chosen have the opportunity to act. He puts people and situations together. How people act in a situation is up to them, though God often prompts His children to know what to do. God will not force or coerce. Persuasion, long-suffering, and love unfeigned mark His leadership style and provide the beacon for us to follow.

## Charismatic Leadership

On rare occasions a truly unusual leader arises who is more than a master of situations. Such *rara aves* not only anticipate and control situations but actually create totally new opportunities. They see the world in new and refreshing ways and create novel approaches to the definition and solution of problems. They create order out of disorder. They draw others to them. Such unusual people possess one of the most powerful forms of leadership—charisma.

*Charisma* is a word of Greek origin that translates as "gift of divine grace." It may be defined as "a certain quality of an individual personality by virtue of which he [or she] is considered extraordinary and treated as endowed with supernatural, superhuman, or at least specifically exceptional, powerful qualities." (Max Weber, *On Law in Economy and Society,* as quoted by Perry W. Buffington, "Star Quality," *SKY,* September 1990, p. 101.)

The followers of charismatic leaders are lifted up, given new visions of what they can do or become, raised to new heights of conduct and aspiration. Both the leader and the followers are elevated or exalted. In the process, followers increase their own capacities and activities. They become leaders themselves.

7

Charismatic leaders possess three driving attributes: power, passion, and purpose. (See Laura Hall Rose, *Charisma: Power, Passion and Purpose* [Buffalo, N.Y.: Bearly Limited Press, 1991].) Their power may arise from rank or position but ultimately is a personal mantle that is almost tangibly present. People feel good to be around them, believing they will gain some of the leaders' personal power by being in their presence. The passion of charismatic leaders — their intense belief in what they are trying to do — is transmitted to others who pick it up and share in it to the extent that they may even feel the leaders' dream or vision is their own. Charismatic leaders also possess a deep and abiding sense of purpose, a vision of an ideal future state that is presented as inevitable. This sense of inevitability, of following an immutable, divinely ordained timetable, is well illustrated in Joseph Smith's famous statement: "No unhallowed hand can stop the work from progressing; persecutions may rage, mobs may combine, armies may assemble, calumny may defame, but the truth of God will go forth boldly, nobly, and independent, till it has penetrated every continent, visited every clime, swept every country, and sounded in every ear, till the purposes of God shall be accomplished, and the Great Jehovah shall say the work is done." (*History of the Church* [Salt Lake City: Deseret Book Co., 1970], 4:540.)

President Spencer W. Kimball is the best example I know of a charismatic leader, though Winston Churchill's World War II leadership in Britain also comes readily to mind. President Kimball was a "star of the first magnitude," as President Ezra Taft Benson called him (*Ensign*, December 1985, p. 33), a man of great spiritual depth and insight, one who sought the will of the Master in all matters affecting the Church and had the courage and faith to accept the manifestation of that will. The Church and the Latter-day Saint people were transformed by his leadership, lifted to new heights of performance, and given a glimpse of what can be done if we will but "lengthen [our] stride," "quicken [our] pace," and "extend [our] vision."

President Kimball's historic impact on the Church and the world is perhaps all the more noteworthy because it was at least partially unexpected. He succeeded a man of unusually dynamic personality and obvious spiritual stature, Harold B. Lee. President Kimball was older than President Lee and had experienced a number of difficulties with his health. Some there were, both in the Church and out, who felt perhaps that President Kimball's administration would be a period of consolidation, of marking time, an *interregnum* of sorts. Of course, the Church would survive, but some unknowing observers wondered how effectively Spencer Kimball could lead it onward and upward.

It didn't take long for opinions to change. On the morning of April 4, 1974, President Kimball addressed the General Authorities and regional representatives from around the world. After a few preliminary remarks, he got down to the meat of his message, and a new awareness fell on his listeners. Elder W. Grant Bangerter spoke of what happened next:

> We became alert to an astonishing spiritual presence, and we realized that we were listening to something unusual, powerful, different from any of our previous meetings. It was as if, spiritually speaking, our hair began to stand on end. Our minds were suddenly vibrant and marveling at the transcendent message that was coming to our ears. With a new perceptiveness we realized that President Kimball was opening spiritual windows and beckoning to us to come and gaze with him on the plans of eternity. It was as if he were drawing back the curtains which covered the purpose of the Almighty and inviting us to view with him the destiny of the gospel and the vision of its ministry.

9

I doubt that any person present that day will ever forget the occasion. I, myself, have scarcely reread President Kimball's address since, but the substance of what he said was so vividly impressed upon my mind that I could repeat most of it at this moment from memory. . . .

President Kimball spoke under this special influence for an hour and ten minutes. It was a message totally unlike any other in my experience. I realized that it was similar to the occasion on the 8th of August, 1844, when Brigham Young spoke to the Saints in Nauvoo following the death of the Prophet Joseph. Sidney Rigdon had returned from Pittsburgh, where he had apostatized, to try to capture the Church. Many people testified, however, that as Brigham Young arose, the power of the Lord rested upon him to the extent that he was transfigured before them, with the appearance and the voice of Joseph Smith. That moment was decisive in the history of the Church, and the occasion of April 4, 1974, is parallel.

When President Kimball concluded, President Ezra Taft Benson arose and with a voice filled with emotion, echoing the feeling of all present, said, in substance: "President Kimball, through all the years that these meetings have been held, we have never heard such an address as you have just given. Truly, there is a prophet in Israel." (*Conference Report*, October 1977, pp. 38–39.)

Only one example of many that could be cited will be given to illustrate President Kimball's unusual qualities of charismatic leadership. I refer to the revelation on priesthood, received in June of 1978, which indicated in an unmistakable manner that the time had come to extend the priesthood to all worthy men, regardless of race or color. I have written elsewhere (*The Dawning of a Brighter Day* [Salt Lake City: Deseret Book Co., 1990], chapter 4) of some of the events surrounding that revelation, which President

Benson termed "one of the most significant in this dispensation." (*Ensign,* December 1985, p. 34.) Clearly, a matter of divine timing was involved, and the Lord Himself was the author of the revelation. But we must not forget the significant role played by President Kimball in importuning and supplicating the Lord, in seeking His will with unwearying diligence (see Helaman 10) and demonstrating the humble obedience to follow the Lord's voice.

News of the revelation on the priesthood flashed through the Church like a bolt of high-voltage electricity, opening new visions of the brotherhood of man and new understanding of the worldwide mandate of the Church to bring *all* to Christ. The vast majority of the Saints quickly accepted the exalting vision of a universal priesthood of all worthy men and rejoiced in President Kimball's inspired leadership.

Readers may say, "That's all very interesting, but President Kimball was the Lord's prophet and entitled to special help. I'm not fashioned out of the same heroic mold he was! I don't have his talents." No doubt about it, President Kimball *was* an unusual spiritual giant. Be assured, however, that *all* leaders in the Lord's kingdom are entitled to that same spirit of revelation that inspired, motivated, and transformed President Kimball into a true shepherd-leader. The Savior made that clear in numerous startlingly powerful references to His desire to help us become more effective leaders in His cause. To illustrate, consider the power contained in these promises:

> That which is of God is light; and he that receiveth light, and continueth in God, receiveth more light; and that light groweth brighter and brighter until the perfect day. (D&C 50:24.)

> Behold, I stand at the door, and knock: if any man hear my voice, and open the door, I will come

11

in to him, and will sup with him, and he with me.
(Revelation 3:20.)

I will be on your right hand and on your left,
and my Spirit shall be in your hearts, and mine
angels round about you, to bear you up. (D&C
84:88.)

Within the context of this discussion, I understand
these scriptures to indicate not only the Savior's willingness to help us but also His burning desire to do so. Note
also that the promise extends to *all*. It is not limited to
those who hold high positions in the Church. The deacon's
quorum advisor is as entitled to receive divine assistance,
within the bounds of *his* responsibilities, as is the president
of the Church in *his* assigned areas of responsibility.

"But my talents are mediocre at best," someone may
complain. "I just don't have the capacity to do the work."
Nonsense! God knows what you can do far better than
you know it yourself. After all, you are one of His children!
He knows you have the capability. You may have much
to learn; you may need to be taught and trained; but your
capacity to do the work, if you choose to do so, cannot be
doubted. God knows both your heart and your mind. Don't
forget, President Kimball didn't become a prophet over-
night. His talents were developed over time, during many
years of humble service, here a little and there a little. So
it must be with all of us. There is no royal road to righteousness. Each must pay the price for spiritual growth.
It is never easy, but then, if it were, it wouldn't be worth
having!

## Leadership "In the Lord's Way"

Because God's leaders must necessarily differ from
those of the world, too much attention to worldly leadership styles is unlikely to prove very fruitful for the Lord's
shepherds. They must look elsewhere for a description of

12

the tasks before them and what is expected if they are to act in "the Lord's way."

At the end of the day, where do they turn to find the most appropriate description of the essential elements of great leadership? At first glance, Joseph Smith's famous dictum "I teach them correct principles and they govern themselves" may seem deceptively simple — too simple, perhaps, to capture the elusive essence of leadership. However, this succinct statement goes to the very heart of a powerful definition of great leadership.

Students of human behavior tell us that, in Western societies at least, we simultaneously seek gratification of two deep-seated psychological needs: the need for a sense of group unity (which brings security) and the need for independence. Paradoxically, these two needs are in opposition to each other. Each of us wants to excel — to stick out from the rest — and at the same time to possess a transcending set of values that unites us with others. We want to be the same as others, but, at the same time, we struggle to be different.

Great leaders help those they lead meet both these fundamental needs. They provide the opportunity to those they lead to stick out, to excel, to determine their own destinies, to govern themselves. At the same time, they combine that freedom with a system of values and beliefs that provides transcending and exalting meaning to life and unites the person concerned with other believers. Teaching correct principles, as found in the scriptures and the words of the living prophets, provides individuals with the common set of values and beliefs necessary to bind them together with others as a people. Letting them govern themselves provides individuals with the opportunity to control their own destiny. Both basic psychological needs are met simultaneously. Teaching correct principles and then letting the people govern themselves thus is a powerful prescription for leadership "in the Lord's way." Indeed, that leadership style truly *is* the Lord's way.

The Savior taught and retaught the great principles that must govern our thoughts and actions if we are to inherit eternal life. However, He does not command in all things but lets us govern ourselves. Jesus' words to the Prophet Joseph come to mind: "It is not meet that I should command in all things; for he that is compelled in all things, the same is a slothful and not a wise servant. . . . Men should be anxiously engaged in a good cause, and do many things of their own free will . . . for the power is in them, wherein they are agents unto themselves." (D&C 58:26–28.)

While these verses clearly speak to the need for people to show initiative and energy in fulfilling their callings, they should also remind leaders of the fact that people are agents unto themselves and capable of governing themselves if they are taught correct principles.

There is another reason why letting people govern themselves is a powerful leadership tool. People who feel they control their own destiny, at least in part, persist at assigned tasks. They become more committed to them and do better at them. Leaders who allow little or no initiative on the part of counselors or teachers, who tell them exactly what must be done, every step of the way, do little to foster the commitment essential for significant accomplishment. Those who are assigned goals under such circumstances are liable to feel no real sense of obligation to achieve them. Their attitudes are likely going to be those of a counselor in a presidency I once knew. "Those aren't *my* goals," he'd say when handed a detailed list by his president. "You haven't even discussed them with me. If you feel so great about them, why don't *you* accomplish them?" Commitment comes with ownership, and ownership comes from participating in the setting of goals, from leader and follower "reasoning together" (see Isaiah 1:18) in deciding what needs to be done and how to do it. Wise shepherd-leaders know and practice that principle.

## Accountability

There is, of course, a great difference between letting people govern themselves and standing by while either nothing is done or dangerously wrong things are done. No shepherd can permit someone for whom he or she has responsibility to fail to take the needed action, or, what is even worse, act in ways that hurt others or hinder the furtherance of the Lord's work through ill-advised initiatives. Thus, a wise leader insists on accountability, not in a threatening or coercive way but in recognition of the fact that unless people feel accountable, they are not liable to feel committed. Once a goal is decided upon, progress toward its achievement must be periodically evaluated. Otherwise, the one to whom the goal's achievement has been assigned may feel that the goal isn't important. After all, if it were, the leader would care enough to ask for an accounting.

Wise shepherd-leaders recognize that accountability is a fundamental law of celestial management: "It is required of the Lord, at the hand of every steward, to render an account of his stewardship, both in time and in eternity. For he who is faithful and wise in time is accounted worthy to inherit the mansions prepared for him of my Father." (D&C 72:3–4.)

Paul the apostle knew of the importance of accountability. In his letter to the Galatian Saints he wrote of the law of ultimate accountability, the law of the harvest: "Whatsoever a man soweth, that shall he also reap." (Galatians 6:7.) That law applies in the moral sphere, of course, but it is also a powerful reminder of the direct

15

cause-and-effect relationship between other aspects of behavior as well.

President Kimball was a great practitioner of the principle of accountability. One of my colleague General Authorities recounts how President Kimball taught him that lesson in a sweet, gentle, but never-to-be-forgotten way. As my friend remembers:

> Soon after I was called, President Kimball asked to see me. Amongst other questions and directions he asked if I kept a personal journal. Somewhat shamefacedly I had to admit I hadn't up to that point. I pled the pressures of a busy professional life. President Kimball didn't chastise or berate me. Gently and lovingly, he reached over and patted my hand. "Please, good brother," he said, "start to keep a journal, starting today."
>
> Several months went by. One day I had a telephone call from President Kimball. "Would it be convenient for you to drop by my office for a few minutes?" he asked. "Oh, and bring your journal with you."

When leader and follower participate jointly in determining goals, both share responsibility for their achievement. The follower, of course, has the major responsibility to ensure that the goal is met; but the leader must stand ready to assist as required to ensure that the follower does not fail. Elder Victor L. Brown tells of a young deacons quorum president who understood well that principle. The young man "startled his adult leaders by asking a boy who hadn't been coming to church to offer the prayer in quorum meeting. When asked afterwards if it was really wise to ask a boy to pray who had only been in church the second time, he responded, 'But I just spent three days this week teaching him how to pray.' " (*Ensign,* November 1989, p. 77.) Youth can be wise beyond its years!

It is worth reiterating that goals are necessary; but if

people are to govern themselves, they must have a hand in setting goals for which they are responsible and in determining ways to achieve them. The extent of that involvement will necessarily vary with the situation and the person concerned. Those with a proven "track record" may appropriately receive only broad policy guidelines and be left to fill in the "how-to-do-it" on their own initiative; someone with only limited experience may require an extra measure of guidance. Situations of great importance or sensitivity may require a higher level of involvement by senior leaders. Preparing for a visit by a member of the First Presidency is of a different order than organizing a deacon's social!

Through it all, however, shepherd-leaders should so discipline themselves that they avoid giving unnecessary, detailed instructions that serve only to annoy and frustrate. I think of a stake Relief Society president who learned that lesson the hard way. She and her counselors planned an opening social, which was all very straightforward except that the president didn't know when to leave well enough alone. She assigned one of her counselors to be responsible for the program and the other for the refreshments. Then, instead of letting the counselors do their jobs within agreed-upon guidelines, she proceeded to undermine the work of the counselor assigned to look after refreshments. She did so in two ways. She began to make her own assignments for specific parts of the refreshment "package," without any reference to the assigned counselor and without her knowledge. Furthermore, she gave the counselor no room for personal initiative at all. The president even decided — arbitrarily — that apple juice and not orange juice, or any other liquid refreshment for that matter, would be served. Her motives, of course, were good. She wanted to ensure a successful event. But her actions guaranteed there would be problems. And so there were. Frustration, ruffled feelings, threats of resignation — all followed. It was an unhappy affair that would never have occurred had the president understood her role properly.

## Balancing Supervision and Freedom to Act

Shepherd-leaders need both courage and wisdom to properly balance the amount of supervision needed to ensure that necessary performance levels are achieved without intruding on the moral agency of others. In no aspect of leadership is that more difficult to achieve than in dealing with youth, where the difference between "shadow" and "wet-blanket" leadership can be hard to define and even more difficult to control. Wise shepherds may be prepared to accept less-than-perfect performance in the short run in order to teach lessons that will have long-term payoffs.

A young women's leader was repeatedly assured by the class president that a social event for the Laurels was well in hand. "Don't worry," the Laurel class president said several times. "I'm looking after everything." But she wasn't. Only two days before the event, to which parents had been invited, nothing at all had been done by way of preparation. The adult leader had several choices: She could step in, brush the Laurel class president aside, do the work herself, and salvage the whole operation. Or she could do nothing and just let the program crash. A third option would have her provide advice and help to stave off disaster but still honor and maintain the overall responsibility of the Laurel class president and her associates. "If I step in and take over responsibility," the leader reasoned, "we'll probably have a high-class event; but the class president will have learned that I'll bail her out whenever she has trouble. That just teaches irresponsible behavior. On the other hand, if the event flops completely, the Laurels will all be embarrassed — and in front of their parents, too." Wisely, the leader recognized that the best

18

option was to prevent total failure but help the class president learn that if you don't prepare, you won't succeed. She provided some help and advice but made certain responsibility for the event remained where it had been assigned, with the Laurel class president. The young woman learned her lesson—the next event was planned and executed properly.

## Teaching Correct Principles

Teaching correct principles to others requires not only a knowledge of what is taught but also a dedication to the principles concerned. Speaking of President Brigham Young, James B. Allen has written: "A man becomes a leader not only because of his ability to organize, persuade, and direct activities of others with diverse attitudes and abilities, but also because of his devotion to the unifying ideals of the particular group involved." (James B. Allen, *The Man—Brigham Young* [Provo, Utah: Brigham Young University Press, 1968], p. 23.)

Throughout Brigham Young's life, there were two unifying ideals that guided, directed, and sustained him. The first was the great latter-day work of the Restoration— the principles and practices of Mormonism, so-called, centering on the redeeming sacrifice of Jesus Christ and the restoration of His gospel to the earth for the last time. Second, President Young possessed a deep and touching fidelity, an unwavering devotion, to the Prophet Joseph Smith. The two ideals were inseparably connected in his mind. He was utterly convinced that Joseph Smith was God's prophet and instrument in the restoration of saving truths to the earth. He said:

> Joseph Smith has laid the foundation of the kingdom of God in the last days; others will rear the superstructure. . . . I know that he was called of God, and this I know by the revelation of Jesus

19

Christ to me, and by the testimony of the Holy Ghost. Had I not so learned this truth, I should never have been what is called a "Mormon," neither should I have been here to-day. (*Journal of Discourses* 9:364–65.)

Brigham Young knew full well "the business of the Latter-day Saints" and the Prophet's part in it all:

I feel like shouting hallelujah, all the time, when I think that I ever knew Joseph Smith, the Prophet whom the Lord raised up and ordained, and to whom He gave keys and power to build up the kingdom of God on earth and sustain it. These keys are committed to this people, and we have power to continue the work that Joseph commenced, until everything is prepared for the coming of the Son of Man. This is the business of the Latter-day Saints, and it is all the business that we have on hand. (Ibid., 3:51.)

Those who wish to prepare themselves for the shepherd's task in the Lord's church must burn with the same conviction of the principles involved as did President Brigham Young. That is the prerequisite for true leadership. You cannot teach others principles you do not believe yourself. Acquiring a profound knowledge and conviction of those principles, and conveying them with power and passion to others, is the work of a lifetime.

## The Leader As Steward

Stewardship, a feeling of deep responsibility to act as the Lord's agent, is perhaps the highest attribute of leadership, the distinguishing mark of the greatest leaders. It is more an attitude than anything else. Its roots lie in the concept of service, and of leaders as servants. In his book *Servant Leadership: A Journey into the Nature of Legitimate Power and Greatness*, Robert K. Greenleaf explained stewardship as follows: "The servant leader *is* servant first. . . .

It begins with the natural feeling that one wants to serve, to serve *first*. This conscious choice brings one to aspire to lead. That person is sharply different from one who is *leader first*." ([New York: Paulist Press, 1977], p. 13.)

In a real sense, therefore, the greatest leaders do not see themselves as such. They seek only to serve, with no desire for self-aggrandizement or acclaim. They see themselves as the Lord's servants, on His errand, acting as His agents, imbued with a deep sense of responsibility to further His interests rather than their own. The scriptures speak repeatedly of the sacred responsibility God places upon His servants to act as faithful agents or stewards. (See, for example, Genesis 26:5; Matthew 20:8; 25:14–29; Luke 16:2; and Titus 1:7.) The word of the Lord given through the Prophet Brigham Young seems particularly appropriate for our time: "Thou shalt be diligent in preserving what thou hast, that thou mayest be a wise steward; for it is the free gift of the Lord thy God, *and thou art his steward.*" (D&C 136:27; italics added.)

Over what, then, are the Lord's servant-leaders to be stewards? The answer is simple: over *all* that He has given them—every material blessing, every talent, every responsibility.

The Lord expects His servants to be diligent in furthering His cause. He expects them to carry out their duties in all faithfulness, with an eye single to His glory. His anger is kindled against those who are slothful, who fail to act as faithful servants. This sober reminder of responsibilities is well illustrated by the following story recounted many years ago by Elder Reed Smoot:

> I remember, when I was a small boy, President Brigham Young was making one of his tours and arrived at a town in one of the southern counties. He had intended to stop there and speak to the people, but, as he drove along the streets, entering

21

town, he noticed the unclean condition of the sur-
roundings. He drove direct to the Bishop's home,
stopped his team and said to the Bishop, who stood
in front of his residence waiting the arrival of the
president: "Why Bishop, I see the same old rocks
upon the streets; I see the same old dirty surround-
ings; I see the same old gates off their hinges; I see
the same old broken down fences; I see the same
old puddles of mud before the tithing office and
your public buildings, just as they were when I was
last here; and, inasmuch as I called attention to
these defects when I was here before, and it has
had no effect upon the people whatever, I do not
think it necessary for me to stop this time. Good-
bye, Bishop. Tell the people when they attend to
these things and rectify them, I will stop next time.
(*Conference Report,* April 1903, p. 53.)

Of even greater importance than responsibility over
possessions is the charge God gives to His servants to care
for the lambs of His flock. In a stirring address at general
conference in April 1966, Elder Marion D. Hanks, himself
a great shepherd, spoke movingly of the grave responsibilities shepherds have to be stewards in the Lord's kingdom. He recounted a tender story about a young woman
whom he called Donna (though that was not her real name)
who left her home in a small town to seek employment in
a large city. She failed to find work, became discouraged
and lonesome, and fell under the influence of an unscru-
pulous and designing man. He led her into an immoral
experience. Donna, heartsick at what had happened, returned home to tell her mother and her bishop of the
tragedy. She began to learn the sorrow of a remorseful
conscience, followed by the blessings of gratitude for God's
grace and mercy. Then Donna found she was pregnant.
She decided to remain at home to await the birth of her
baby. In Elder Hanks's words:

Donna stood up in the next fast and testimony

22

meeting and explained her condition. She acknowledged her fault and asked the forgiveness of her people. She said to them, "I would like to walk the streets of this town knowing that you know and that you have compassion on me and forgive me. But if you cannot forgive me," she said, "please don't blame my mother—the Lord knows she taught me anything but this—and please don't hold it against the baby. It isn't the baby's fault." She bore testimony of appreciation for her bitterly won but dearly treasured personal knowledge of the importance of the saving mission of Jesus Christ. Then she sat down.

The man who told me the story reported the reaction of the congregation to this experience. There were many tearful eyes and many humble hearts. "There were no stone throwers there," he said. "We were full of compassion and love, and I found myself wishing that the bishop would close the meeting and let us leave with this sense of appreciation and concern and gratitude to God."

The bishop did rise, but he didn't close the meeting. Instead he said, "Brothers and sisters, Donna's story has saddened and touched us all. She has courageously and humbly accepted full responsibility for her sorrowful situation. She has, in effect, put a list of sinners on the wall of the chapel with only her name on the list. I cannot in honesty leave it there alone. At least one other name must be written—the name of one who is in part responsible for this misfortune, though he was far away when the incident occurred. The name is a familiar one to you. It is the name of your bishop. You see," he said, "had I fully performed the duties of my calling and accepted the opportunities of my leadership, perhaps I could have prevented this tragedy.". . .

"My brothers and sisters," he said, "I don't know how long I am going to be bishop of this ward. But as long as I am, if there is anything I can do about it, this won't happen again to one of mine."

The bishop sat down in tears. His counselor stood up and said, "I love the bishop. He is one of the best and most conscientious human beings I have ever known. I cannot leave his name there on the list without adding my own. You see, the bishop did talk with his associates. He talked with me about this matter. I think that he thought that because I travel occasionally in my business through the big city, I might find a way to check on Donna. I might have done, but I was hurrying to this meeting or that assignment and I didn't take the time. I too talked with others. I mentioned my concern to my wife. I am almost ashamed to tell you I talked to the Lord and asked him to help Donna. And then I did nothing. I don't know what might have happened had I done what I thought to do, but I have the feeling that I might have prevented this misfortune. . . ."

The president of the YWMIA stood up and told a similar story. The bishop's counselor in charge of this auxiliary organization had talked with her. She had had some moments of thought and concern but had done nothing. She added her name to the list.

The last witness was an older man who stood and added two names to the list—his own and that of his companion ward teacher. He noted that they were assigned to the home in which Donna and her mother lived and that they had failed in some visits and made no effective effort to be the kind of teachers that the revelations of God had contemplated.

"I don't know how long I will be a ward teacher," he said, "but as long as I am, I will not miss another home another month, and I will try to be the kind of teacher that the Lord seemed to have in mind." (*Conference Report*, April 1966, pp. 151–52.)

In addition to all else for which they are responsible,

faithful stewards also have a deep sense of personal commitment to the mission of the Church. They see that mission in personal terms, as one that applies directly to them and for which they bear a *personal* responsibility. They know that someday the Master will demand of them an accounting of what they did in helping to bring to pass the immortality and eternal life of man. They mobilize the most noble force of their souls and give their full commitment to a cause greater than any earthly, mortal responsibility—that of proclaiming the gospel, redeeming the dead, and perfecting the Saints—that all may come unto Christ.

In fulfilling his or her sacred stewardship, a wise shepherd believes strongly that the example of a single life *can* make a difference, touching hearts and influencing many lives for good. A story from the early days of the Restoration illustrates the point. In April 1836, Elder Parley P. Pratt arrived in Hamilton, Ontario, on a missionary journey from Kirtland, Ohio, to upper Canada. He was penniless and could not pay the two-dollar fare for a lake steamer to take him the thirty miles to his destination of Toronto. As was his custom, Elder Pratt importuned the Lord. Shortly thereafter a stranger gave him ten dollars.

Upon arriving in Toronto, Elder Pratt went to the home of John Taylor, whose name and address had been given to him by a business acquaintance of Taylor's. Taylor, an English immigrant to Canada and lay preacher in the Methodist Church, had heard many derogatory remarks about the Mormons. At first he would have nothing to do with Elder Pratt. Within a few weeks, however, Taylor became convinced, after thorough study, that Elder Pratt spoke the truth. John Taylor and his wife Leonora were baptized on May 9, 1836. John Taylor later became the third president of the Church.

Soon after he was baptized, Brother Taylor went with

Elder Pratt to call on a Mr. Joseph Fielding, who lived a few miles away. Fielding had two sisters, young women who, seeing the two visitors coming, ran from their home to a neighbor's, lest they should give welcome or even acknowledgment to "Mormonism." Joseph Fielding joined the Church and within the year accompanied Elder Heber C. Kimball to England to open up missionary work there. Mary, one of Joseph's sisters, would later become the wife of Hyrum Smith and the mother of Joseph F. Smith, sixth president of the Church, and grandmother of Joseph Fielding Smith, tenth president of the Church.

John Taylor's wife, Leonora Cannon, came from the Isle of Man. Her nephew, George Q. Cannon, was baptized as a boy of twelve years by Elder Taylor in 1840, during his second missionary journey to England. George Q. Cannon later emigrated to America. He became an apostle and a counselor in the First Presidency under presidents Young, Taylor, Woodruff, and Snow. All this from a single missionary journey! (See Francis M. Gibbons, *John Taylor: Mormon Philosopher, Prophet of God* [Salt Lake City: Deseret Book Co., 1985].)

# CHAPTER TWO

# Watching Over the Flock

Perhaps the term that best describes the personality of Jesus is one He applied to Himself. "I am the good shepherd," he said, "and know my sheep, and am known of mine." (John 10:14.) To the pastoral peoples of ancient times, those of the flock and field, Jesus' remarks struck a responsive chord. The shepherd was a familiar sight to them. He stayed with his flock both day and night (Luke 2:8), led the flock to fresh pastures each morning (John 10:3–4), carefully and tenderly watched over each member during the day, and ensured that all were safely within the sheepfold when evening came. Equipped with a curved staff for guiding the sheep, a rod used as a weapon, and a sling (Psalm 23:4; 1 Samuel 17:40), he was prepared to defend the flock against predators such as bears or lions (1 Samuel 17:34–35; John 10:11–13), to give his life, if need be, to protect those in his charge. Yet he willingly left the ninety and nine to go out into the wilderness, seeking the one that was lost. (Luke 15:4–6.) The shepherd was an honored figure.

The symbolism of Christ as Shepherd is referred to repeatedly in the scriptures. The psalmist sang, "He is our God; and we are the people of his pasture, and the sheep of his hand." (Psalm 95:7.) Using the same powerful symbolism, Isaiah wrote, "He shall feed his flock like a shepherd: he shall gather the lambs with his arm, and carry them in his bosom, and shall gently lead those that are with young." (Isaiah 40:11.) Said faithful Nephi, "He gathereth his children from the four quarters of the earth; and he numbereth his sheep, and they know him; and there shall be one fold and one shepherd; and he shall feed his sheep, and in him they shall find pasture." (1 Nephi 22:25.) Successful leaders in the Lord's Church look upon themselves as His undershepherds, blessed to help Him care for the flock of Christ, sharing the responsibility to watch over every member.

One of the great tragedies of life occurs when a sheep or lamb who has come to Christ drifts away from the sheepfold of God. Some become inactive, others critical or prone to find fault. A few precious souls fall prey to ravenous revilers who call evil good and good evil. (Isaiah 5:20.) Serious transgressions may even result in some forfeiting their Church membership. In each who leaves, the flame of faith falters and grows faint under the ashes of indifference or sin. To all who for whatever reason have drifted away, the First Presidency addressed a loving message in late 1985: "Come back," they said, "Come back and feast at the table of the Lord, and taste again the sweet and satisfying fruits of fellowship with the Saints. . . . We plead with you. We pray for you. We invite and welcome you with love and appreciation." (*Ensign*, March 1986, p. 88.)

No part of the leader-shepherd's role is more important than that which takes him or her out into the highways and thickets of the world to find and bring back members of the flock of Christ who have wandered away, in whom the fire of faith and testimony has dimmed and grown cold. As leaders do so, theirs is the joy expressed so beautifully by the Savior in that powerful parable found in Luke 15: "What man of you, having an hundred sheep, if he lose one of them, doth not leave the ninety and nine in

28

the wilderness, and go after that which is lost, until he find it? And when he hath found it, he layeth it on his shoulders, rejoicing. And when he cometh home, he calleth together his friends and neighbours, saying unto them, Rejoice with me; for I have found my sheep which was lost." (Luke 15:4–6.)

Sad to say, it is, and probably ever will be, the tendency of some to stray from the fold of the Good Shepherd. As Elder James E. Talmage wisely said, "History fails to present any example of great undertakings upon which multitudes enter with enthusiasm, and from which many do not desert." (*The Great Apostasy* [Salt Lake City: Deseret Book Co., 1968], p. 23.)

Finding lost sheep and loving them back into full fellowship with the Saints must, therefore, be seen as an intrinsic, eternal part of the shepherd's role. Faithful shepherds for all seasons understand that winter or summer, year in and year out, finding, bringing back, and tenderly caring for the sheep are among the tasks the Lord expects His undershepherds to carry out.

The scriptural reminder that "the worth of souls is great in the sight of God" (D&C 18:10) takes on new meaning to those involved in finding lost sheep and helping to rekindle their faith. The joy felt in heaven when a lost child is found and brought back is echoed in the hearts of faithful, caring undershepherds. These shepherds say that many who have left the fold come to realize that life without Christ is a perpetual twilight. The shepherds also speak of loving parents who pray that someone will find a prodigal son or daughter, of tears of joy and gladness at rediscovery, and of the prodigal's reawakened desire to sup again at the table of the Lord. It is a great miracle.

Yet the greatest miracle of all is not the finding of those who are lost. Rather, it is the ability of the Savior's love to heal and make whole, to apply a balm of Gilead to sin-

29

sick souls, to restore to full understanding precious truths long since hidden by the cares of the world and the wiles of the wicked.

Why does Christ welcome back those who have been lost? Why does He call upon His undershepherds to go out into the wilderness of the lone and dreary world to find and bring back those in whom the fire of faith has grown cold? The answer is both simple and profound. The Savior exhorts us to do so because He loves all mankind, seeing in each of us an eternal worth that flows from our divine inheritance as the sons and daughters of God: "He inviteth them all to come unto him and partake of his goodness; and he denieth none that come unto him, black and white, bond and free, male and female; . . . and all are alike unto God." (2 Nephi 26:33.)

Wise shepherd-leaders understand that the distinction between "shepherd" and "sheep" is neither constant nor distinct. For example, a priesthood leader, whom one would normally think of as serving in a shepherd's role, may under some circumstances move from giver to receiver of blessings. During a lifetime we oscillate repeatedly between being nurturing shepherds and nurtured sheep. That fact underlines our mutual interdependence — for we are *all* "the people of his pasture, and the sheep of his hand." (Psalm 95:7.) We are responsible for each other — not as our brother's keeper, but as brothers and sisters freely "willing to bear one another's burdens . . . and comfort those that stand in need of comfort." (Mosiah 18:8–9.) We cannot escape that responsibility nor expect someone else to accept it for us. At the end of the day a willingness to love and serve one another is the hallmark of our Christian discipleship and of our devotion to God.

Among those in whom the fire of faith has grown cold, faithful undershepherds find souls with special burdens — the lonely; single parents; those who are aged, ill, or troubled; those from broken homes. For them, the shepherds must provide special, tender care. Unfortunately, history records that the shepherds have sometimes not reached out in love and tenderness to those whose needs are greatest. Of such the Prophet Jeremiah intoned: "My people hath been lost sheep: their shepherds have caused them to go astray; they have turned them away on the mountains: they have gone from mountain to hill, they have forgotten their restingplace. . . . Israel is a scattered sheep." (Jeremiah 50:6, 17.)

Through the prophet Ezekiel the Lord reproved those shepherds who do not feed the flock:

> Son of man, prophesy against the shepherds of Israel, prophesy, and say unto them, Thus saith the Lord God unto the shepherds; Woe be to the shepherds of Israel that do feed themselves! should not the shepherds feed the flocks? . . . Ye feed not the flock. The diseased have ye not strengthened, neither have ye healed that which was sick, neither have ye bound up that which was broken, neither have ye brought again that which was driven away, neither have ye sought that which was lost; but with force and with cruelty have ye ruled them. And they were scattered, because there is no shepherd. (Ezekiel 34:2–5.)

The results that will almost certainly occur if shepherds fail to care for the sheep are presented in the following apocryphal "Parable of the Lost Sheep":

> When the shepherd findeth it he layeth it not on his shoulders. Neither bringeth he it back to the sheepfold. He feedeth it not; yea, he provideth neither grain nor hay. Cool clear water he bringeth not. And the sheep starveth. Yea, it wasteth away. He bindeth not up its wounds; he applieth no balm to its blemishes. In its weakness and hunger the sheep crieth for help. But he stoppeth up his ears.

Its entreaties he heareth not. Then cometh the
wolves, and carrieth the sheep away. Then sayeth
the shepherd to his friends: "Did I not tell you the
sheep was good for nothing?"

Circumstances change during life, and someone who
has previously been indifferent or even cold toward the
Church may experience a change of heart over time. The
Savior's words come to mind: "Ye know not but what they
will return and repent, and come unto me with full purpose
of heart, and I shall heal them; and ye shall be the means
of bringing salvation unto them." (3 Nephi 18:32.) I think
of a woman, baptized in 1930, long inactive, who when
contacted in 1968 said that she and her husband and son
had attended another church for many years and were
happy with that arrangement. She was found again by the
Lord's shepherds twenty years later. In the interim her
husband had died, and her attitudes had changed. She
now was very friendly, wanted contact with the Church,
and desired home teachers. She still had her copy of the
Book of Mormon! Significantly, the missionaries were led
to her through her nonmember brother.

That leads me to reiterate one of the cardinal characteristics of newly found sheep: the flame of faith in them
dies hard. Often it can be fanned back to life, even though
covered with the ashes of apparent disinterest. The wise
words of President J. Reuben Clark come to mind:

It is my hope and my belief that the Lord never
permits the light of faith wholly to be extinguished
in any human heart, however faint the light may
glow. The Lord has provided that there shall still
be there a spark which, with teaching, with the
spirit of righteousness, with love, tenderness, with
example, with living the gospel, shall brighten and
glow again, however darkened the mind may have
been. And if we shall fail so to reach those among
us of our own whose faith has dwindled low, we

shall fail in one of the main things which the Lord expects at our hands. (*Conference Report,* October 1936, p. 114.)

A story told by wonderful, loving missionaries illustrates the enduring truth of President Clark's words. Wrote one of them:

> We located a man who was quite gruff and unfriendly as he came to the door. He demanded to know how we had found him and what we were doing there. He wanted nothing to do with the Church. Despite our attempts to reason with him, the good brother remained adamant and bitter in his desire not to have membership in the Church. In his anger he wrote a letter to the Bishop, then and there, demanding that his name be removed from the records of the Church.
>
> As we were walking towards our car, I continued to speak to the man about the importance of the gospel in our lives. I bore my testimony of the truthfulness of the gospel and what it has done to benefit the many who have made the effort to live its principles and keep the commandments of God. I could see tears welling up in his eyes. I admonished him to pray, study the scriptures and think seriously of what he had just done. I pointed out that he could still rescind the letter if he wished. Following a few moments of silence he said softly, "You'd better hold the letter for a while to give me time to think."

How great is the power of pure testimony!

Many who have strayed from the fold of Christ had no real intention of doing so. Some drift away in the first few critical weeks or months after baptism, when they are still so tender and vulnerable. The flame of their faith grows faint more by neglect than anything else. Two examples illustrate the point:

A former missionary, on a return visit to his field of

labor, tried to locate people he had baptized nearly a quarter-century ago. He found a man, baptized by him twenty-three years earlier but lost a short time after his baptism. "When you left soon after my baptism," the newly found sheep recounted, "I hadn't been in the Church long enough to withstand the temptations of the world. Nobody else helped me, and I soon drifted away. But I still know the gospel is true."

Another man, baptized years ago and long since lost, told a similar story when he was found again. "Before I got a chance to learn," he said, "the missionaries left, and I thought the members didn't care. I quit going to Church after a few weeks, even though I had a testimony. I still know that the feelings I had at baptism were the whisperings of the Spirit. The gospel is true." Now, more than a quarter-century later, the man contemplates what might have been. His nonmember wife, who had not objected to his baptism, has left him, and none of his three children are members either. Sheep who become lost may take others with them, including lambs not yet born.

Some members drift away because they lack the courage to proclaim their faith to an apostate world. Fearing "man more than God" (see D&C 3:7), they become "ashamed of the gospel of Christ" (Romans 1:16). In their fear they stray away, and they may take others with them. They are in special need of a loving hand to lift them up and rekindle their faith. Another missionary example will illustrate:

> One sister we met had been only partially active for over thirty years. There was never any doubt in her mind about the truthfulness of the Church, but her husband forbade her from "getting too involved" and certainly she was not to allow any Mormons to visit their home. One day her husband informed her she could again return to limited ac-

tivity, but only on Sunday. There was to be no weekday participation and certainly no special projects or programs to claim her time! She felt this mood change would surely be of short duration, but she went cautiously about her return to activity. She said little, but her feelings of happiness and inner peace were very difficult to hide. Not knowing the sensitivity of her home situation, we unwisely visited her without an appointment. She was obviously very concerned when she saw us, and her husband made no attempt to hide his displeasure. We noted a picture of three beautiful children on the mantelpiece and quickly determined one cannot go wrong talking about a person's grandchildren. Forty-five minutes later as we prepared to leave, everyone was relaxed and speaking freely about many subjects. Equally as important, we had an invitation to return—extended by the husband.

A week or so later as we visited with this dear sister, she could hardly contain her feelings of happiness. She related that a few days following our visit to their home, her husband asked if he could speak with her on a very important matter. He began by saying: "I think it is about time I had a talk with the Bishop to learn if my baptism of thirty-five years ago is still valid. If so, maybe I'd better begin to honor it."

This good brother and his family had moved into the area many years earlier, and he had never acknowledged being a member of the Church. He had warned his family to maintain silence regarding his membership. His withdrawal from activity, according to him, was caused by the two-pronged problem so often expressed by less-active members: failure to be adequately taught the gospel, and failure in fellowshiping. We visited several times with this brother and listened attentively and tearfully as he related the anguish of more than thirty years of fear and false pride that had prevented him from returning to Church even though he knew the gospel was true.

One wonders if he sensed something impending, because his change of attitude and desire to return to full fellowship were cut short by his death in less than two month's time. His loving, patient, long-suffering wife has expressed the comfort she feels knowing he really did believe but needed help to return.

Another important lesson for shepherd-leaders to keep in mind about newly found souls is that many—perhaps most—of them know little about the gospel. Lack of knowledge clearly is a factor in their inactivity. The fire of faith and testimony soon falters if not fed. Repetition is required for learning. Few who have drifted far away have experienced that frequent referral to the principles of the gospel needed to drive essential truths into the soul to the point where behavior begins to change. Few are familiar with the scriptures, those powerful witnesses of Christ. (See John 5:39.) Their knowledge of the saving and redeeming truths found in the Book of Mormon is especially deficient. In a word, most require conversion. Without conversion, activation is fleeting and superficial. These perceptive words from Alma 23:6 say it best: "As many as believed, or . . . were brought to the knowledge of the truth . . . and were converted unto the Lord, never did fall away."

The responsibility that falls upon shepherds to ensure that those who hear are brought to a knowledge of the truth through spirit-directed teaching is obvious. Those who attend priesthood quorums and auxiliaries and gospel essentials classes must feel the Spirit and experience the joy and edification it brings. (See D&C 50:17–23.)

To be effective, efforts to find and bring back those who are lost must be both organized and personalized. True shepherds know that each sheep is different from all others, with unique strengths, weaknesses, hopes, fears, and talents. Personalized love must be an overarching principle that unifies all that is done.

In a recent testimony meeting, a lovely sister expressed the joy she and her husband felt when they joined the Church more than fifteen years earlier. A few months after their baptism, the missionaries who had taught them and to whom they felt especially close completed their missions and returned home. Soon doubts, fears, and uncertainties began to gnaw at the new converts, as old habits and old friends began to lure them away from the fold of Christ. She explained that they were saved from a slow slide into inactivity only because a couple in their ward loved and cared for them. Many evenings were spent discussing gospel principles and Church procedures. Aid was given in replacing old friends with new ones. The new converts were encouraged to accept Church callings and helped to be successful in carrying them out. Prevention carried out early in their Church life obviated the need for redemption later on. The sister concluded her testimony: "We sometimes went to Church when we didn't particularly want to, but we knew our friends loved us and we grew to love them. That love has become deeper as we realize more each day what they did for us."

In summary, then, finding, bringing back, and caring for lost sheep and lambs are tasks of supernal significance assigned by the Good Shepherd to faithful undershepherds. In their accomplishment is found some of the richest joys of work in the Master's cause. How thrilling it is to brush away the ashes of apathy, indifference, even antagonism, to reveal and revive the faintly glowing ember into a flickering flame of faith. Those so involved can exult with Ammon, "My heart is brim with joy, and I will rejoice in my God." (Alma 26:11.)

An example from secular history illustrates the importance of shepherd-leaders taking their job seriously. It is a tragic story, one that ended in unmitigated disaster. It is told here, not out of love for blood and gore, but to illustrate a great truth: the sheep look to the shepherds for example and counsel. When the shepherds fail, the sheep suffer.

On the 6th of January, 1842, under unremitting pressure from Afghan mobs, the British army that had occupied the city of Kabul, Afghanistan, for several months began its retreat to the safety of the garrison at Jalalabad. It was the beginning of the most terrible rout in the history of British arms, a tragedy so monstrous and final as to be unparalleled in all of Britain's long martial experience.

The army and those who followed it had to travel only ninety miles; but it was in the midst of the bitter Afghan winter, through wild mountain terrain choked with snow and infested with thousands of intensely hostile tribesmen. Disorderly, already confused, some 16,500 souls struggled out of Kabul, leaving behind a plundering, screaming mob that burned the British cantonment before those who left it were out of sight. The marchers—if they could be called that, since they soon became a muddled, terrified, undisciplined mass—were comprised of some 700 British soldiers, 3,800 Indian sepoys, and more than 10,000 camp followers and their children and servants, both British and Indian. Almost within the hour, stragglers began to drop out of the line of march, and soon the trail was littered with a grisly collection of dead and dying people, abandoned baskets, boxes and cooking pots, dead bullocks and horses.

The retreat lasted just a week. The struggling mass, which had long since ceased to resemble a disciplined group of soldiery, shrank steadily in number. Each gully hid an ambush; each ridge was topped by a line of marksmen who poured a fury of musket fire on the passersby. Frostbitten, snowblind, without food or ammunition, the

38

survivors struggled on, their ordeal made the more horrible by the piercing cold of the Afghan winter.

By the 13th of January the destruction was complete. Thirteen British soldiers (twelve of them officers) had been taken prisoner, as had thirteen British women and sixteen children. Apart from a few wandering Indian sepoys, there remained but a single uncaptured survivor—Surgeon Brydon of the Army Medical Corps. Tormented by Afghan horsemen, who chopped at him with their sabers and pelted him with rocks, he spurred his exhausted horse over the last few miles to Jalalabad.

Suddenly, Brydon found himself alone. His tormentors faded away into the gloom of the early afternoon, content no doubt that there should be one survivor who could provide details of the butchery that had occurred. Far in the distance Brydon saw the high mud walls of Jalalabad, with the Union Jack fluttering in the breeze above them. Slumped over the neck of his horse, he weakly waved his cap. The gates of the fortress opened, and men ran to lift him from his trembling animal. And so the retreat from Kabul came to its terrible end. (Adapted from *Heaven's Command*, the first volume of James Morris's trilogy on the British Empire [New York: Penguin Books, 1979], pp. 86–112.)

There are many in the Church who, like those who retreated from Kabul, fall victim and are lost. Why is this so? Some are seduced and led away by the temptations of the world, betrayed and weakened by its false promises. Bereft of the protection of "the whole armour of God," they soon fall beneath the onslaught of evil that surrounds us on all sides.

A few, perhaps, are frozen by the indifference and lack of love shown by Church members. Their enthusiasm cools, their ardor for the gospel becomes sluggish, and soon they too drift away and are lost. Like the army that

fled Kabul, some lack the discipline needed to stick together, to draw strength and courage from each other, to
hang on and persevere to the end. Their courage falters
in the face of criticism from old friends and the seductive
allure of old habits. Losing their grip on the iron rod, they
fall away into the mists of darkness, not to be seen again.

Finally, there are others, cut and bleeding from a thousand blades of misfortune, who simply give up and cease
to struggle. Life with its inevitable disappointments and
unfulfilled dreams overwhelms them, and, like dry leaves
caught in a mountain torrent, they are swept away.

The task of the Lord's shepherd-leaders is to prevent
the spiritual reenactment of the retreat from Kabul. Those
who are entrusted with the shepherding role must work
with all diligence to provide the love and care needed to
protect the Saints from spiritual marauders who dart in to
pick off stragglers. They must ensure that all share in the
warmth of the gospel of Christ. Theirs is the task to shelter
the weak and weary, give courage to the faint-hearted,
instill the discipline needed to withstand the world, and
strengthen the feeble knees.

Paradoxically, perhaps, shepherds will find the
strength to turn aside the fiery shafts of the adversary only
as they become as little children. The scriptures tell us to
become "submissive, meek, humble, patient, full of love,
willing to submit to all things which the Lord seeth fit to
inflict upon [us], even as a child doth submit to his father."
(Mosiah 3:19.) The arm of flesh will not suffice. The ferocity
of the natural man will not win the necessary battles, for
"the natural man is an enemy to God, and has been from
the fall of Adam, and will be, forever and ever, unless he
yields to the enticings of the Holy Spirit, and putteth off
the natural man and becometh a saint through the atonement of Christ the Lord." (Mosiah 3:19.)

It must be emphasized that, unlike those who bled and

died in the retreat from Kabul, we "wrestle not against flesh and blood, but against principalities, against powers, against the rulers of the darkness of this world, against spiritual wickedness in high places." (Ephesians 6:12.) Now is the day of Satan's power on earth. In every land he attempts, with fiendish skill and considerable success, to subvert and thwart the work of God. Malignant, treacherous, and cunning, his power grows daily.

To withstand Satan and his legions of dupes and devils, shepherd-leaders must put on "the whole armour of God." They must have "[their] loins girt about with truth, and [have] on the breastplate of righteousness; and [their] feet shod with the preparation of the gospel of peace; above all, taking the shield of faith, wherewith [they] shall be able to quench all the fiery darts of the wicked. And [taking] the helmet of salvation, and the sword of the Spirit, which is the word of God." (Ephesians 6:13–17.)

The retreat from Kabul must be seen as a tragic failure of shepherding. Taken as a group, the British officers, who should have set the example as shepherds of the flock, failed miserably at their task, preferring to save their own skins rather than putting the safety of their men first. The senior British commander, General William Elphinstone, was described by one of his major subordinates as "the most incompetent soldier that was to be found among the officers of the requisite rank."

It is noteworthy that other than Surgeon Brydon, who was not captured, twelve of the thirteen surviving British troops were officers. In fairness, four of the officers were taken as hostages under protest, at the order of the senior officer present, General Elphinstone. Nonetheless, overall, the actions of the officers involved represent a terrible indictment of shepherds who abandoned their flock.

Contrast the behavior of the army that retreated from Kabul with that of the beleaguered Martin and Willie hand-

41

cart companies in the American West. Of course, we must be cautious and careful in making the comparison, since the two groups faced very different problems. Nevertheless, the actions of the handcart pioneers and of the shepherds who led them, and those who found and saved them, were markedly different from the actions of those who fled Kabul.

The story of the Martin and Willie companies is one of the most pathetic yet inspiring in the history of the Church. Its main outlines are well known to members of The Church of Jesus Christ of Latter-day Saints, though little recognized by others. It is a story of heroic dimensions, an epic of courage, endurance, and faith in God, that will live forever in the annals of the kingdom.

They were an improbable lot of heroes, those handcart pioneers; and, of course, they never considered themselves as such. As Wallace Stegner said of them, "They looked more like the population of the poor farm on a picnic than like pioneers about to cross the plains." ("Ordeal by Handcart," *Colliers*, July 6, 1956, p. 79.)

Like the army that fled from Kabul, they, too, had their ordeal in the snow. Unlike those who struggled across the Afghan wilderness, however, there was among the handcart pioneers no panic, no hysterical terror, no loss of group cohesion. Through all of their hardships they stayed together, helping each other, sharing grief and burdens, burying their dead as best they could, and moving on, ever westward. Their shepherds did not fail them but shared equally in their sorrows and travail, helping as best they could.

Of course, the handcart pioneers were not hounded and harassed by hostile tribesmen as was the Kabul army. Perhaps that explains why they held together and did not break. Yet somehow I doubt it. After they had lost their discipline and became a rabble instead of an army, those fleeing Kabul had only their fear to bind them together. The handcart pioneers, on the other hand, were bound together by the deep bonds of a common religious faith that gave them a sense of mutual obligation, of shared brotherhood and sisterhood. Thus sustained by their deep and abiding faith in God, they were prepared to pay whatever price was required of them to gather to Zion. Even years later, none of them was bitter over the terrible experiences. All deemed it a privilege to have had that opportunity to become "acquainted with God." (*Relief Society Magazine*, January 1948, p. 8.)

Wallace Stegner summed up well the accomplishments of the handcart companies when he wrote, "If courage and endurance make a story, if human kindness and helpfulness and brotherly love in the midst of raw horror are worth recording, this half-forgotten episode of the Mormon migration is one of the great tales of the West and of America." ("Ordeal by Handcart," *Colliers*, July 6, 1956, p. 85.)

Effective leadership necessarily involves proper preparation. All true shepherds understand that. Failure to prepare in war is an almost certain guarantee of disaster. The British army at Kabul paid a terrible price because of its lack of preparation. Long before the first of the mobs assembled, there were plenty of signs that major trouble was brewing in the city. Senior British officials were murdered. Rumors abounded for months of threatened rebellions, of secret meetings where dark deeds were planned, of tribesmen assembling out of sight and sound of the foreigners. But the British seemed lost in a dream world of their own making. They did nothing. The officers refused to see what was staring them in the face. They seemed unwilling or unable to detect the almost palpable evidence of an impending crisis, and even less willing to do anything about it. Thus, they were not ready for the hammer blows that struck them.

Let us then resolve there will be no retreats from Kabul in the Church. Let us develop our shepherding skills so we can serve as effective guardians over those for whom the Lord has given us stewardship responsibilities. Let us ever be alert to their needs and wise and perceptive in helping keep them safe from the spiritual marauders who menace the tender souls in our care.

The scriptures tell us that "if ye are prepared ye shall not fear." (D&C 38:30.) Preparation is as important for religious leaders as for those who lead an army or govern a nation. Shepherds who do not prepare almost guarantee they will not achieve desired results. Opportunities for spiritual progress will be lost. Precious lambs will wander away from the flock, perhaps never to return.

Some there are who may quote scripture in an attempt to prove that preparation is not necessary. "Take [no] thought beforehand what ye shall say . . . and it shall be given you in the very hour that portion that shall be meted unto every man," they intone. (D&C 84:85.) Such faulty logic, far from proving that preparation is not necessary, indicates merely the pitfalls that await those who quote scripture preferentially and incompletely. Inclusion of the words left out in the above-noted quotation clarifies the matter. Verse 85 of section 84 reads in its entirety: "Neither take ye thought beforehand what ye shall say; *but treasure up in your minds continually the words of life*, and it shall be given you in the very hour that portion that shall be meted unto every man" (italics added). The phrase "treasure up in your minds continually the words of life" obviously implies preparation, without which we will have precious little to treasure up! "Be Prepared" is the Scout motto. How aptly it applies to shepherd-leaders!

Preparation permits two factors to influence our decisions: judgment and the Spirit. Combining the two permits us to exercise effective leadership. Wise shepherds will strive constantly to be prepared in two general ways: spiritually and technically. Both are hard work, requiring long hours and unremitting effort. Both call for concentration, commitment, and courage. Both demand discipline and determination.

The fruit of spiritual preparation is an endowment of power from on high—the power necessary to supplement our natural abilities, to strengthen the arm of flesh. "Sanctify yourselves and ye shall be endowed with power . . . yea, purify your hearts, and cleanse your hands and your feet before me," the scriptures say. (D&C 43:16; 88:74.) Personal purification is the price we must pay for spiritual preparation. We must be washed clean of the soil and dross of the world. "Be ye clean, that bear the vessels of the Lord." (Isaiah 52:11.) We must yield our hearts unto God if we desire sanctification. (See Helaman 3:35.) To know God requires that we give away all our sins. (See Alma 22:18.)

Prayer, fasting, pleading, importuning—all are involved. Striving each day that we live to mirror the Master in our thoughts and actions is necessary. To follow Him we must learn of Him. "Search the scriptures," He said, "for they are they which testify of me." (John 5:39.) As we learn of Him, as we draw closer to Him, as we strive to become like Him (see John 14:21), we grow in spiritual power. We become more effective shepherds, more valuable servants.

Fundamental to spiritual preparation is the setting of proper priorities. "Seek ye first the kingdom of God," the Savior taught. (Matthew 6:33.) Leaders who do not place Him first simply cannot succeed in His work. They become mere herders of sheep rather than true shepherds, hirelings rather than trusted stewards. Speaking of the prophet who would be favored at some future date to bring to light the buried Nephite record, Moroni pointed out that "none can have power to bring it to light save it be given him of God; for God wills that it shall be done with an eye single to his glory." (Mormon 8:15.) Shepherds, if they are to be spiritually prepared, must therefore learn to set priorities that accord to the Lord His proper place in their lives.

Spiritual preparation is not something once done and forever finished. It must be seen as a process rather than an event—a lifelong commitment demanded by our discipleship. The long process of trial and training must itself be recognized as a test of our faith. Perseverance, patience, and enduring to the end are required. Painful, distressing times of anguish and adversity come to all. God has promised none of us an easy ride. But He has promised us a greater gift, the capacity to overcome, and the strength to endure. Only as we pass through the refiner's fire can we progress toward perfection.

Successful shepherds know that failure to prepare themselves technically will limit their effectiveness. Success does not come to those who fail to do their homework. Good intentions are not enough. Sincerity will not suffice. Even God has difficulty inspiring an empty mind. Said Brigham Young, "We are trying to teach this people to use their brains. . . . Whatever duty you are called to perform, take your minds with you, and apply them to what is to be done." (*Journal of Discourses,* 11:328; 8:137.) Oliver Cowdery, who mistakenly thought that revelation came without effort, without thought "save it was to ask," was taught that "you must study it out in your mind; then you must ask me if it be right." (D&C 9:7-8.)

Studying it out in the mind can be hard work. Many of the problems faced by the shepherds of the Church are complex and difficult. Often shepherds are required to choose between shades of gray. Nor should they delude themselves into thinking that there is only one God-or-dained solution to each of life's problems. The truth is that sometimes He is indifferent as to how we choose. "It mattereth not unto me," He pointed out to undiscerning disciples who wished to know the details of how they should travel to their homes. (D&C 60:5.) Under such circumstances He expects us to do "as seemeth [us] good" and to get on with it!

Service to others is the hallmark of the life of the Lord's shepherd-leaders. It is the highest expression of Christian stewardship. Service to others drives out selfishness, the great enemy of spirituality. Subduing the ego permits soul growth and signifies the extent of our devotion to Christ and His cause. It is the mark of true greatness of character. Jesus knew that and exemplified it in His life. Said He, "Whosoever will be great among you, let him be your minister; and whosoever will be chief among you, let him be your servant." (Matthew 20:26–27.)

History reflects numerous examples of men and women who wore out their lives in service to others. One such person was Florence Nightingale, the founder of the modern nursing profession. Born in 1820 in Florence, Italy, where her well-to-do British parents were temporarily resident, she grew to womanhood in England. A child of privilege, she could easily have spent her life in the mindless pursuit of pleasure. But she was made of sterner stuff. She felt deeply that God had a mission for her to accomplish. She trained in Germany as a practical nurse and became the superintendent of nurses at a hospital in London. It was not an easy task. Nursing at that time was a profession with little prestige to which women of good character and breeding were not attracted. In 1854, when war broke out in the Crimea between Britain and France on the one side and Russia on the other, Florence took a party of nurses to work in the military hospitals to which the wounded were brought.

When she arrived at the hospital in Scutari, Turkey, Florence found that wounded men were being kept under appalling conditions of filth, degradation, and gross overcrowding. The walls were thick with dirt; the floors rotten. Vermin scurried everywhere. There were no basins, no towels or soap, insufficient bedding and bandages. Characteristically, Florence's first requisition was for 200 scrub brushes.

Blessed with an iron will and unflinching courage, Florence fought the hostility of the medical establishment and the army bureaucracy to obtain supplies needed for proper nursing of desperately wounded soldiers. She reorganized the kitchens and laundries. Prodigious efforts were made to clean the wards and bring to their inhabitants some of the amenities of civilized life. The wounded began to receive nourishing, well-cooked food and the comfort of clean linen. Wounds were dressed regularly, and the men were bathed and given clean clothing.

Florence drove herself hard. She worked eighteen-hour days, making her rounds through the wards late at night, a lamp in her hand, giving comfort and solace to thousands. She became idolized by the soldiers, who called her "The Lady with the Lamp." They kissed her shadow as it passed and scrupulously watched their language in her presence. Her unstinting service paid off. In a few months the mortality rate among the wounded fell from more than 42 percent to 22 per 1,000.

Florence became a national hero in her native Britain. But she cared little for personal glory, refusing public transport home and every kind of public honor. She was more interested in obtaining improved living conditions for the soldiers. Important and wide-ranging reforms resulted from her efforts.

In 1860 she organized the Nightingale Training School for Nurses at St. Thomas' Hospital in London, the first of its kind in the world. The justly honored position held by the nursing profession today throughout the world has resulted in no small measure from the example of Florence Nightingale's extraordinary life of unstinting service. I believe she would have agreed with King Benjamin, who knew that "when ye are in the service of your fellow beings ye are only in the service of your God." (Mosiah 2:17.) (For further information regarding this extraordinary woman, see Lytton Strachey's perceptive essay "Florence Nightingale" in his book *Eminent Victorians* [London: Penguin Books, 1948].)

Faithful shepherd-leaders place great emphasis on service to others. The fruits of that service are found in souls who come to Christ, in lives that are changed for the eternities. Consider the following letter, written on February 3, 1857, by Charles F. Jones, president of the Birmingham England Conference, to Elder Parley P. Pratt. In the letter, President Jones gives an accounting of his stewardship over a portion of the Lord's sheepfold. It is an outstanding example of what can be done, under the most humble of circumstances, by diligent, faithful shepherd-leaders who seek only to serve, succor, lift, and love.

> When I took charge of this Conference, I found it in a good condition, with the exception of a debt, which was caused through the heavy expenses upon it the previous year. But I am pleased to say that at the end of the year 1856, it was entirely out of debt. And although in the previous year more was paid than in any former one, I am proud to say that £300 more has been paid, for various purposes, this year than last, which proves that the faith of this people is on the increase. To be brief I will say that they have paid for various purposes the sum of £1877.

This amount has been used in paying back debts; General Conference expenses; assisting Elders in going to Zion; contributions to the Temple and Emigration Funds; support of Priesthood; relief of poor, etc.

In addition to this the Saints have paid on behalf of their own Emigration the sum of £429 3s. 7d.

We have also disposed of books and *Stars* to the value of £262 1s. 6d.; making a total of £2631 5s. 1d.

We have 146 Elders and 133 Priests; the majority of these men have been employed during the past year in distributing tracts, and preaching in and out of doors. . . . During the year we have baptized 298 persons . . . [and] 178 persons left for Utah. The Conference is now in a healthy condition, numbering 1516 . . . [with] ten Sabbath schools . . . where [children] are taught to read, write, etc., with good effect. (*Millennial Star*, 19:141–42.)

Service may require apparent sacrifice. In our congregations we often sing a great hymn about the prophet Joseph Smith that contains the memorable line "Sacrifice brings forth the blessings of heaven." ("Praise to the Man," *Hymns*, no. 27.) That sacrifice may take many forms, from the physical hardships suffered by the early pioneers to social ostracism and the loss of employment, friends, or even family associations. For many the greatest apparent sacrifice is giving up the things of the world—unbridled ambition, a love of power or possessions, sensuality in all its diverse forms; all of the sins that keep us from communion with God. Those who yield "their hearts unto God" (Helaman 3:35), who are willing to give away all their sins to know him (see Alma 22:18), soon find that what they have given up was no sacrifice at all. They feel no sense of loss but rather a deep rejoicing in the knowledge that their feet are planted firmly on the path that leads to broad sunny uplands of celestial joy.

President Marion G. Romney understood well the importance of sacrifice in the attainment of celestial joy. Said he:

> When earth life is over and things appear in their true perspective, we shall more clearly see and realize what the Lord and his prophets have repeatedly told us, that the fruits of the gospel are the only objectives worthy of life's full efforts. Their possessor obtains true wealth — wealth in the Lord's view of values. . . . I conceive the blessings of the gospel to be of such inestimable worth that the price for them must be very exacting, and if I correctly understand what the Lord has said on the subject, it is. The price, however, is within the reach of us all, because it is not to be paid in money nor in any of this world's goods but in righteous living. What is required is wholehearted devotion to the gospel and unreserved allegiance to the Church of Jesus Christ of Latter-day Saints. . . . There can be no . . . reservation. We must be willing to sacrifice everything. Through self-discipline and devotion we must demonstrate to the Lord that we are willing to serve him under all circumstances. When we have done this, we shall receive an assurance that we shall have eternal life in the world to come. Then we shall have peace in this world. (*Conference Report,* October 1949, pp. 39, 43–44.)

Yes, sacrifice, though it tugs at our heartstrings and stretches us almost beyond what we think we can bear, does indeed bring forth the blessings of heaven.

## *Applying the Principles: Guidelines for Shepherds*

Faithful undershepherds strive diligently to serve those for whom they have divinely directed responsibility. It is a difficult task, one that could not successfully be carried out without the Lord's help. Demands placed on the time, energy, and abilities of even well-trained and highly motivated shepherds simply exceed mortal abilities. That may seem a presumptuous statement; after all, many men and women in the secular world are superbly successful in operating large-scale business and public organizations. But to do the Lord's work requires more power than that provided by the arm of flesh. Advanced degrees or extensive experience in business or public administration, though perhaps useful, will not suffice and are not really all that important. An extra endowment of spiritual power is required. (See D&C 43:16.) The following guidelines are presented to help shepherds obtain that power "in the Lord's way."

1. *The faithful shepherd knows each sheep personally and cares for each one individually, as his or her friend.* The shepherd sees in each member of the flock a child of God, of enormous—even infinite—value. (See D&C 18:10.) Just getting to know some of the sheep can be both time-consuming and difficult. It is not even easy to find some members of the flock! Not all are equally hospitable or open-hearted. Some hide shyness or feelings of inadequacy or pain behind a gruff demeanor. A few may appear cold or disinterested. I well recall going many years ago as a home teacher to visit a man who would not even acknowledge my presence for several months. He was and had been totally inactive for twenty years or more. His first impulse was to completely ignore the home teachers, I suppose in hopes they would go away. After several months, though, he began to open up, and his unfriendly, even hostile, demeanor gave way to cheerful friendliness. I can't report that he came back to Church, but at least contact was made and friendships formed.

Knowing every sheep personally requires shepherds to develop the divine gift of discernment. Though this gift is conferred upon all people generally through the light of Christ (Moroni 7:16–18), the Lord's shepherds receive additional power through revelation from the Holy Ghost (D&C 46:16) to discern what is in the hearts of the members of their flock.

The spirit of revelation rested upon the prophet Samuel as he set about to select one of the sons of Jesse as a successor to Saul, who had forfeited his right to the office of king through willful disobedience. Samuel thought to himself as he looked on Eliab, the eldest son, "Surely the Lord's anointed is before [me]." But the Lord said unto Samuel, "Look not on his countenance, or on the height of his stature; because I have refused him: for the Lord seeth not as man seeth; for man looketh on the outward appearance, but the Lord looketh on the heart." When David the shepherd boy and the youngest of Jesse's sons was brought before Samuel, the Lord said, "Arise, anoint him: for this is he." (1 Samuel 16:6–7, 12.)

Faithful shepherds plead with all their hearts to know the Lord's will for His children. They long for that endowment of power that will permit them to discern what is in the heart of each member of the flock, and they cry to God for the power to provide necessary help and counsel. Prayer, pleading, importuning of the Lord may be required ere His will is known. The Prophet Joseph, who knew well the process involved, indicated the determination and persistence required when he advised, "Come to God, weary him until he blesses you." (Andrew F. Ehat and Lyndon W. Cook, eds., *The Words of Joseph Smith* [Provo, Utah: Brigham Young University Religious Studies Center, 1980], p. 15.)

In seeking to know and care for each member of the flock, faithful shepherds are motivated by charity, the pure love of Christ (Moroni 7:47)—a love that is centered on righteousness such that he or she who possesses it is concerned only with the soul of the recipient. Charity is a spiritual gift, an endowment from the Almighty, bestowed on those who are true followers of Christ (Moroni 7:48), which enables us to love others as the Father and Son love us.

2. *The faithful shepherd numbers the sheep (Moroni 6:4), maintains up-to-date records on each, and accounts for each.* In both ancient and modern times, God has commanded that His covenant people maintain sacred records detailing their lives and relationships to Deity and to each other. Said Alma to Helaman: "I command you that ye take the records which have been entrusted with me; and I also command you that ye keep a record of this people . . . and keep all these things sacred which I have kept, even as I have kept them; for it is for a wise purpose that they are kept." (Alma 37:1–2.) Speaking of the practice followed in the Nephite church in its time of righteousness following Christ's appearance in America, Moroni recorded:

> None were received unto baptism save they took upon them the name of Christ, having a determination to serve him to the end. And after they had been received unto baptism, and were wrought upon and cleansed by the power of the Holy Ghost, they were numbered among the people of the church of Christ; and their names were taken, that they might be remembered and nourished by the good word of God, to keep them in the right way, to keep them continually watchful unto prayer, relying alone upon the merits of Christ, who was the author and the finisher of their faith. And the church did meet together oft, to fast and to pray, and to speak one with another concerning the welfare of their souls. And they did meet together oft to partake of bread and wine, in remembrance of the Lord Jesus. And they were strict to observe that there should be no iniquity among them; and whoso was found to commit iniquity, and three witnesses of the church did condemn them before the elders, and if they repented not, and confessed

54

not, their names were blotted out, and they were not numbered among the people of Christ. But as oft as they repented and sought forgiveness, with real intent, they were forgiven. And their meetings were conducted by the church after the manner of the workings of the Spirit, and by the power of the Holy Ghost; for as the power of the Holy Ghost led them whether to preach, or to exhort, or to pray, or to supplicate, or to sing, even so it was done. (Moroni 6:3–9.)

The practice of "taking the names" of the people and of "numbering" them implies that the shepherds know all the members of the flock individually. Furthermore, following such a practice requires shepherds to consider the unique strengths and weaknesses, challenges and talents of each individual, one by one. Modern-day bishop-shepherds follow that principle when they prayerfully seek guidance for each young man and young woman in the ward, individually rather than collectively. Collective evaluations of people are of little lasting worth. "When we deal in generalities, we shall never succeed," President Thomas S. Monson has wisely stated; but "when we deal in specifics," he adds, "we shall rarely have a failure." Wise leaders use statistics, reports, and lists of the names of members categorized in various ways to consider how best to bless the lives of specific individuals and concentrate resources where they are most needed.

True shepherds know they are accountable for all of the flock, not just for those who are members of the Church. They take special actions to provide the additional help needed by those who pasture on the edges of the flock. What shepherds need most, perhaps, is an attitude of mind that helps them to look to the needs of all, to feel responsible for everyone. The specific actions needed to help a particular individual will soon become apparent once that attitude is firmly implanted in shepherds' hearts.

Of course, prayer and pleading will be required, but God does not leave His servants alone and without promise of divine assistance. One of the sweetest assertions of God's love and support for His servants is found in the Savior's words to the Prophet Joseph Smith as recorded in D&C 84:88: "I will go before your face. I will be on your right hand and on your left, and my Spirit shall be in your hearts, and mine angels round about you, to bear you up." Shepherds who have that assurance can sing with the Psalmist: "I will lift up mine eyes unto the hills, from whence cometh my help. My help cometh from the Lord, which made heaven and earth. He will not suffer [my] foot to be moved: he that keepeth [me] will not slumber." (Psalm 121:1-3.)

3. *The wise shepherd leads the sheep by example, from the front.* How wondrous is the power of example! Jesus, the perfect leader, knew that rear-echelon leadership will not suffice. "Come, follow me," He proclaimed. (See Matthew 4:19; 19:21; John 1:43; 8:12.) His faithful undershepherds must shine with a moral goodness that is an ensign to those whom they lead. Their trumpet must sound clear and true, calling all to battle against "the rulers of the darkness of this world." (Ephesians 6:12.) Their moral strength and integrity must be unsullied and beyond taint or question. Theirs is the responsibility to stand on higher ground, that others may be lifted up.

Great shepherds, who lead by example, burn with excitement for the Lord's work. They are consumed by enthusiasm, as was Paul. Wrote he to the Corinthian Saints: "God, who commanded the light to shine out of darkness, hath shined in our hearts, to give the light of the knowledge of the glory of God in the face of Jesus Christ." (2 Corinthians 4:6.) Alma, who knew the sickness of sin and the cleansing power of repentance, desired to speak with "a voice to shake the earth. . . . I know that which the Lord hath commanded me," he said, "and I glory in it. I do not glory of myself, but I glory in that which the Lord hath commanded me." (Alma 29:1, 9.)

The holy fire that consumes and transfigures the Lord's leaders is contagious. It spreads to others, changing them in turn as they, too, catch the vision of the greatest of all works. They slough off the scales of selfishness and "put on the whole armour of God" (Ephesians 6:11) as valiant soldiers in the army of God.

4. *The wise shepherd is not an absent shepherd but is always with the sheep to love, protect, and nurture them.* History records the calamitous effects of absentee leadership practiced by senior Allied officers during World War I. For the most part, the Allied generals and their staffs lived in coddled comfort in luxurious chateaux safely located in the Flanders countryside miles behind the trenches. From there they sent millions of young men to be killed or wounded, blissfully unaware of the inhuman conditions in which the men were forced to live and fight. The anger of those subjected to such shepherds who did "feed themselves" (Ezekiel 34:2–6) shines through Seigfried Sassoon's bitter poem, "Base Detail."

> If I were fierce, and bald, and short of breath,
> I'd live with scarlet Majors at the Base,
> And speed glum heroes up the line to death.
> You'd see me with my puffy petulant face,
> Guzzling and gulping in the best hotel,
> Reading the Roll of Honour, "Poor young chap,"
> I'd say—"I used to know his father well;
> Yes, we've lost heavily in this last scrap."
> And when the war is done and youth stone dead,
> I'd toddle safely home and die—in bed.
> (*The Penguin Book of First World War Poetry*, 2nd edition, Jon Silkin, ed. [Harmondsworth, Middlesex, England: Penguin Books, 1981].)

This is not to say, of course, that shepherds must attend every meeting, take no vacations, or be on call twenty-four hours a day. Those who do so will "surely wear away"; what they attempt is "too heavy for [them]," and they are "not able to perform it . . . alone." (Exodus 18:14–18.) But wise shepherds never leave the sheepfold untended or the flock uncared for. When unavoidably absent themselves, they ensure that other able undershepherds are available to care for all of the members of the flock. Wise Jethro understood that Moses was "burning himself out" by trying to do too much and needed help if he were to succeed. Jethro's advice to a struggling prophet applies equally to modern-day shepherds:

> Hearken now unto my voice, I will give thee counsel, and God shall be with thee: Be thou for the people to God-ward, that thou mayest bring the causes unto God: and thou shalt teach them ordinances and laws, and shalt shew them the way wherein they must walk, and the work that they must do. Moreover thou shalt provide out of all the people able men, such as fear God, men of truth, hating covetousness; and place such over them, to be rulers of thousands, and rulers of hundreds, rulers of fifties, and rulers of tens: and let them judge the people at all seasons: and it shall be, that every great matter they shall bring unto thee, but every small matter they shall judge: so shall it be easier for thyself, and they shall bear the burden with thee. If thou shalt do this thing, and God command thee so, then thou shalt be able to endure, and all this people shall also go to their place in peace. So Moses hearkened to the voice of his father in law, and did all that he had said. (Exodus 18:19–24.)

Shepherds who understand Jethro's message ensure that counselors, teachers, and others are used wisely to care for the flock when they themselves are absent. The shepherd may be required to leave the ninety and nine and go search for the one who is lost. But he or she will not leave those "at home" unprotected or unfolded as prey to spiritual wolves.

If there is one challenge all shepherds share, it is the continual tug-of-war between tasks and time. We all seem so busy trying to juggle the competing demands of church, family, self, and profession. The work seems never to be done, and the time is so short. For the good of themselves, their families, their friends, and the flock entrusted to them, shepherds must learn to periodically reassess priorities, which should include time for family and personal renewal, to determine anew goals and objectives, and to ask honestly and candidly whether the tasks that keep them so busy are the most important in moving the kingdom forward. It is not easy to ask those questions and act on the answers. There is a certain comfort in being busy!

I well recall an overburdened bishop who said to me, "I just can't take the time to plan; I'm too busy!" I sympathize with him; after all, there are programs to administer, organizations to staff, and procedures to follow. All, of course, are important, but they are not the keystone of effective leadership in the kingdom. Our divine purpose as Church leaders is to serve as the Lord's agents, as undershepherds on His errand, entrusted with the care of His children.

It is so easy for shepherds to fall into the trap of believing their *most* important resonsibility is to be an effective administrator. A recent witty cartoon in the *New Yorker* magazine illustrates the point that the shepherd's role transcends administration. It depicts a nattily dressed man, with briefcase in hand, addressing a flock of sheep. "Your shepherd, Louie, has retired," he says. "I am Mr. Smathers. I will be your grazing-resource coordinator and flock welfare-and-security manager." The point is, of course, obvious. The prime role of a shepherd-leader is to provide spiritual help and guidance, not to be a grazing-resource manager! Make no mistake. Administration is important, but it is even more important to minister to the needs of those for whom we have responsibility.

5. *The wise shepherd teaches the sheep to protect themselves from the wolves of the world by following the commandments and by making and keeping sacred covenants.* Wise shepherds are anchored in the principles of the restored gospel. They are assiduous in teaching the flock from the scriptures and the words of the living prophets, knowing that only the "whole armour of God" will protect against spiritual predators. Wise shepherds recognize that the commandments of God recorded in the scriptures have the power to change hearts and minds and thus to protect against the assaults of the adversary and his legions of dupes and devils. President George Q. Cannon stated: "The Gospel of the Son of God is superior to every system known among men. It feeds the soul with knowledge. It points out with exceeding plainness the path which leads to God. It teaches man his duty to his fellow-man and to his Maker. It gives him understanding concerning the nature of God and the character of the Godhead. . . . Who can place a proper estimate upon this knowledge? In value it is beyond price." (*Gospel Truth*, Jerreld L. Newquist, ed. [Salt Lake City: Deseret Book Co., 1974], 2:11.)

To me one of the most beautiful and powerful aids to everyday Christian living is that found in John 14:21: "He that hath my commandments, and keepeth them," said the Savior, "he it is that loveth me: and he that loveth me shall be loved of my Father, and I will love him, and will manifest myself to him." We signify our devotion to and love for Jesus by the extent to which we keep His commandments. Those who say they love Christ, but who don't strive with all their strength to keep the commandments, signal to others, and most importantly to Him, where their true allegiance lies.

The power of the scriptures to make hearts "burn" is exemplified by the experience of the two disciples who unaware walked with the resurrected Christ on the road to Emmaus. Beginning at Moses and all the prophets, Jesus expounded unto them in all the scriptures the things concerning Himself. After Christ's departure, when their eyes had been opened to the divine glory of their companion, the disciples said one to another, "Did not our heart[s] burn within us while he talked with us by the way, and while he opened to us the scriptures?" (Luke 24:27, 32.)

The commandments then, are the words of eternal life, by whose precepts people everywhere are required to live. (See D&C 84:43–44.) As we obey, we are blessed. Wise shepherds, who know this, do all in their power to teach the flock in their care to follow the commandments.

The prophets proclaim, and the scriptures sweetly certify, that all men and women, if they are to achieve true happiness, must come unto Christ and be perfected in Him. To achieve such supernal joy requires a life of dedication and devotion to duty and Deity, a life of service and sacrifice, a life of keeping the commandments. Such a life is characterized by partaking of holy ordinances and by making and keeping sacred covenants, those solemn, celestial agreements between man and God. Making covenants with His people and with individuals has always been one of the major ways in which the Lord deals with His children. God's people have always been a covenant-making people. Said Jehovah to Moses, speaking of ancient Israel: "If ye will obey my voice indeed, and keep my covenant, then ye shall be a peculiar treasure unto me above all people." (Exodus 19:5.) The Nephite scriptures also are replete with references to covenants. Nephi recorded, "My soul delighteth in the covenants of the Lord." (2 Nephi 11:5.) Indeed, the ancient and modern scriptures testify together that the greatest and most glorious blessings our Heavenly Father has for His children are received by covenant. We serve under covenant and not under compulsion, as Elder Boyd K. Packer has reminded us. (See *Ensign*, May 1987, p. 24.)

A covenant, in technical terms, is a solemn agreement between two parties. With respect to the covenants of the gospel, the parties involved are the Father on the one side and faithful, humble suppliants on the other. The agreements entered into are intended to be binding on both participants. We make specific promises and in return are given specific blessings. God, of course, always keeps His side of the bargain. He cannot do otherwise; His very nature forbids it. Sad to say, however, all too often some of God's covenant people, casual in their commitment, take their obligations and covenantal responsibilities less seriously than they should. In so doing, they trample sacred things under their feet.

If we fail to keep our covenants, we are not worthy of Him whose sons and daughters we are (D&C 98:15), and we are "good for nothing only to be cast out and trodden under the feet of men" (D&C 101:39–40). It is a matter of the utmost seriousness. Our position and place in the eternities will be determined by the extent to which we keep sacred the covenants we make here in mortality. Those who accept sacred covenants have a grave responsibility to honor them. The Lord has said, speaking of those who receive the priesthood and then break the covenant pertaining thereto, "Whoso breaketh this covenant after he hath received it, and altogether turneth therefrom, shall not have forgiveness of sins in this world nor in the world to come." (D&C 84:41.)

There fall upon us two principal responsibilities if we are to keep in full force the covenants we make. The first is faithfulness—a willingness to obey the laws of God, to keep the commandments, to observe the standards of the gospel, to endure in fortitude unto the end. Such a one was Nephi, son of Helaman, who sought with unwearying diligence to know the will of God and to keep His commandments. To him the Lord declared, "Because thou hast done this with such unwearyingness, behold, I will bless thee forever; and I will make thee mighty in word and in deed, in faith and in works; yea, even that all things shall be done unto thee according to thy word, for thou shalt not ask that which is contrary to my will." (Helaman 10:4–5.)

To be faithful is to strive each day to keep the commandments, to hunger and thirst after righteousness, to plead for divine guidance, and to seek for and listen to the still, small voice. To be faithful is to listen to and act upon the admonitions of the prophets, to humbly, obediently, and gladly follow their instructions, remembering that the voice of His servants is the same as the Lord's. (See D&C 1:38.) Faithfulness in keeping the commandments thus is not passive; it is active, joyful, anxious engagement in good causes, reverence for righteousness, an eye single to the glory of God. It embodies both commitment and action, and it must be seen within the context of enduring to the end while steadfastly pushing forward, feasting on the words of Christ. (See 2 Nephi 31:20.)

The second responsibility that falls upon us, if we are to keep our covenants, is to magnify our calling—to honor, exalt, and glorify it and to cause it to be held in greater respect and esteem. We magnify our callings, whatever they are, when we see what we do in the framework and context of God's work, when we recognize that the great latter-day work in which we are engaged is of eternal, galactic importance, part of God's eternal plan for His children, foreseen by Him before the foundations of the world were laid. When we do so, we develop the inner joy of recognizing who we are, of knowing that we are God's sons and daughters, known by Him and beloved of Him. We learn of our relationship to our Redeemer and Savior, God's Almighty Son, and we understand that because He bore our sins on Calvary's cross, we may, on condition of faithfulness, return again to our Father's house.

As we magnify our calling, we go the extra mile; we taste the sweet joys of service—the fabric from which a celestial life is woven. And we desire that our brothers and sisters here in mortality may share in the bountiful blessings of the glorious gospel. At the same time, we go even further—we desire the same blessings for our progenitors beyond the veil. Our hearts thus are turned to our fathers; and we carry out vicarious service on their behalf in the holy temple, reaching out in love and service, in caring and compassion, to free them from spiritual captivity.

It is so easy to confuse position in the Church with righteousness—to embrace the pernicious doctrine that those who administer the Lord's affairs are automatically assured first place in the kingdom. While it is certainly true that the Lord loves and trusts His servants, it is worth repeating that our place in the kingdom is determined by our faithfulness in keeping our covenants, not by the position we hold.

The saving and exalting ordinances of the gospel are inextricably intertwined with the sacred covenants. Indeed, no covenant is given unless it is associated with an ordinance, and vice-versa. Thus, the ordinance of the sacrament is associated with three covenants. As we partake of the blessed tokens of the sacrament, we make the following promises to God:

1. We are willing to take upon ourselves the name of the Son.

2. We will always remember Him.

3. We will keep His commandments.

For His part, God promises that we will always have the Spirit to be with us.

If a covenant is a *sacred promise,* an ordinance is a *sacred act;* an act prescribed by the Savior Himself as one of the conditions upon which we receive the exalting blessings of His atonement. The first essential ordinance is that of baptism — the sacred act that provides entrance into the way leading to the celestial kingdom. The essential ordinances that concern exaltation are given and received in the holy temple. Indeed, the Lord has made it clear (D&C 124:40) that the purpose of building temples is to reveal the ordinances therein. The Doctrine and Covenants (84:19–21) also teaches us that the ordinances of the Melchizedek Priesthood contain the powers of godliness. Incidentally, it is worth pointing out that ordinances, to be effective, must be performed by those who have divine authority to do so. God will not accept from us that which He has not Himself commissioned. In this work, more than good intentions and sincerity are required; a valid authorization from God must be obtained.

6. *The wise shepherd recognizes that sheep are best cared for by several undershepherds working unitedly together.* The wise shepherd calls on priesthood quorums and auxiliaries to organize, plan, and focus their efforts on accomplishing the mission of the Church. He or she is careful not to confuse ends with means. Organizations and quorums do not have a mission of their own, separate from the mission of the Church. All must be correlated toward achieving one mission, with three dimensions: "To bring to pass the immortality and eternal life of man." (Moses 1:39.) Wise shepherds do not compartmentalize the Church. They recognize that each aspect of its mission intermeshes and intertwines with the others.

Wise shepherds use the programs of the Church to meet the needs of the people, to support families and individuals as they strive to carry out the mission of the Church. Much of the correlation necessary to do so should occur in the weekly Priesthood Executive Committee and the Ward Council. The information local leaders need to focus on individuals comes in part from the records that are kept. Wise shepherds look beyond the figures to the individuals they represent and then plan and correlate their efforts to help the individuals involved, using all of the resources of the Church. The spirit of that help should be that expressed in Alma 31:35: "Behold, O Lord, their souls are precious, and many of them are our brethren."

7. *The caring shepherd strives constantly to improve his or her own shepherding skills and works diligently to train and prepare other shepherds.* Wise shepherds know how little they know and are anxiously engaged, day by day, in honing and polishing their shepherding skills. They read widely, placing particular emphasis on the scriptures and the words of the living prophets. They recognize that excessive dependence on television can act as a mental soporific. They learn by observing the actions of other, more experienced shepherds. They routinely self-critique their performance, asking, "How could I have improved?" They ask themselves, "If I had to do it again, what would I do differently?"

Wise shepherds seek daily to understand each member of the flock. They plead for empathy, recognizing that one of the most fundamental psychological needs of all members is the need to be understood and appreciated. The wise shepherd learns to listen and to understand, not to hastily prescribe solutions—something that can be risky and very difficult. This takes training, practice, and patience. Wise shepherds spend a lot of their time in sharpening that skill, knowing that much of their success will depend upon their ability to truly understand and value each member of the flock.

Wise, caring shepherds see themselves primarily as teachers. Their model is not the white knight in shining armor, leading his troops in glorious victory, but that of the humble teacher who helps others grow and gets the greatest satisfaction when pupils surpass the accomplishments of their mentor. Though no mortal can even approach the performance of Jesus, I believe the Savior has a special joy when He sees undershepherds striving and growing in His service.

Jesus, who taught "as one having authority" (Matthew 7:29), was and ever will be the greatest teacher. He provides the perfect model for us to follow as we strive to improve our own teaching skills. We are to teach by the Spirit (see D&C 42:14 and 50:17–22), "according to the office wherewith I have appointed you," the Lord says (D&C 38:23). As we strive to do so, we will receive wondrous blessings of power and comprehension, far beyond our mortal capacities. "Teach ye diligently and my grace shall attend you, that you may be instructed more perfectly in theory, in principle, in doctrine, in the law of the gospel, in all things that pertain unto the kingdom of God, . . . that ye may be prepared in all things . . . to magnify the calling whereunto I have called you, and the mission with which I have commissioned you." (D&C 88:78, 80.)

Wise shepherds recognize the need for physical, mental, emotional, and spiritual renewal. They invest in themselves, knowing that if they don't do so, their effectiveness as undershepherds will decrease. They recognize the need for balance in life and know that to develop only one dimension of their talents is to put all others in jeopardy. They realize, on the other hand, that positive renewal of one of the four basic aspects of life mentioned above will positively affect the others. Thus, a shepherd who takes proper care of his or her physical body through proper diet and exercise will find increased mental, emotional, and spiritual strength and enhanced capacity to do the Lord's work. From that renewal, positive change will flow.

In summary, shepherds who understand their divinely appointed responsibility do all in their power to care for each member of the flock, including those who have wandered away. They work hard to improve their effectiveness, knowing that their ministry requires both discipline and determination. They prepare themselves in all things that they may magnify their callings and justify the sacred appellation of undershepherd.

# CHAPTER THREE

# The Communicating Shepherd

In his book *The Discoverers,* Daniel Boorstin describes the difficulties encountered by travelers attempting to trade but unable to speak each others' language. In ancient times, Muslim traders from North Africa, after traversing the Atlas mountains southward, would arrive after many days at the shores of the Senegal River in West Africa. There they would lay out on the ground separate piles of salt, beads and other trinkets, and inexpensive manufactured goods. They would then retreat out of sight. The local tribesmen, who were gold miners and lived in the workings, would appear and put a heap of gold beside each pile of trade goods. Then they in turn would get out of sight, leaving the traders either to take the gold offered for a particular pile or to reduce the amount of merchandise to suit the offered price of gold. Once again the traders would withdraw, and the process would go on until both sides were satisfied.

This bizarre game, conducted in utter silence by both sides, was the best that could be managed by people who could not talk to each other, a "silent trade" carried out in total isolation. (See Daniel J. Boorstin, *The Discoverers,* pp. 160–61.)

Unfortunately, there are still many who practice the modern equivalent of the "silent trade": families who don't talk together, leaders who don't communicate expectations or convey appreciation, shepherds who act as if they were tongue-tied, sheep who seem deaf. No part of the shepherd's task is more demanding or rewarding than that of communicating with the members of the flock. It is, of course, a two-way process, with joint responsibilities to give and receive information. But true communication involves much more than just a transfer of information. It requires a listening heart, the ability to diagnose before we prescribe, to seek first to understand and then to be understood.

## Seek First to Understand, Then to Be Understood

This phrase, an extension of the famous words attributed to St. Francis of Assisi ("O divine Master, grant that I may not so much seek . . . to be understood as to understand . . . ") lies at the heart of true communication. Seeking for understanding is the product of a wise and loving heart, of humility and commitment to service. Its enemies are ego and selfishness, an arrogant self-assurance that assumes *I* know best and others had better listen to *me*. The importance of seeking first to understand was brought home forcefully to me at the start of my service as a General Authority. My first long-term assignment was as a counselor to Elder Jack H. Goaslind, then president of the United Kingdom/Ireland/Africa Area. I well recall the first meeting of the newly assigned Area Presidency. "Brethren," said Elder Goaslind, "the stake presidents and other priesthood leaders here know far more about their challenges and successes than we do. Our job for the first three months is to listen and pray and ponder. Let's not prescribe solutions until we understand the problems."

Over the next three months we did exactly that, talking to every stake president in the Area and visiting every part of it, from John O'Groats to Cape Town. Everywhere we went, we tried hard to *really* listen, to look beyond the

THE COMMUNICATING SHEPHERD

words to what was really meant, to read "body English" as well as the Queen's English. Priesthood leaders, as they found we really wanted to learn and were slow to judge, opened their hearts *and* their minds to us. I'm confident we were much more effective than we would have been had we steamed in with all guns firing, providing answers before we even understood the problems. I'll always be grateful to Elder Goaslind for his wise and humble leadership and great example.

## *Listen with the Spirit*

When we listen with the Spirit, we strive above all else to understand the other person, to get inside his or her head and heart, so to speak, to *really* know what is being said, perhaps without words. This requires not only careful *listening* but also careful *observing*. In fact, the experts tell us that words account for only about 10 percent of communication, with 60 percent coming from "body language" and 30 percent from the tone and inflection of the voice. Listening with the Spirit thus requires far more than just hearing and processing words. It requires close observation of facial expressions, of gestures, of body stance and movement. I recall interviewing a senior priesthood leader and his wife. Sensing that all was not well in their lives, I questioned him closely about specific aspects of his stewardship and relationship with his wife. He insisted there were no problems, none at all. Everything was proceeding just as it should, or so he claimed. Then I glanced at his wife. She, too, insisted there were no problems in their relationship, not a one. Her face, however, betrayed her real feelings. Tears were welling up in her eyes and running down her cheeks. Of course there were problems! Fortunately, they were solvable. He had grown careless about his relationship with his wife and somewhat insensitive to her needs and anxieties. He was and is a good man, striving to be righteous and totally devoted to magnifying his calling and maintaining the honor of a famous name. As occurs with many, however, dedication had slipped over into obsession, and his priorities needed readjustment. Fortunately, once he understood the problem, he was quick to make amends.

Although listening with the Spirit requires the development of skills, more than skill is involved. At its base, listening with the Spirit requires a deep, genuine desire to understand another human soul. Its roots thus lie in character, in service and humility, not in skill. Nor is listening with the Spirit mere sympathy. Indeed, it may not involve sympathy (which implies agreement) at all. Commitment to try to understand is involved, not agreement. Sincerity is essential. Most people quickly comprehend if they are being manipulated and are repelled by behavior perceived as deceitful or self-seeking. Under such circumstances most just "clam up" and won't reveal their true feelings. To do so would be too dangerous, too risky. Indeed, listening with the Spirit *is* risky for both parties involved. Both must be open, both must lower their guards and reveal their true selves. Both must be open to be taught and hence to be changed. Considerable self-assurance is required on both sides.

In its essence, listening with the Spirit is a mutual teaching process in which all parties participate equally. The scriptures tell us what happens under such circumstances: "He that receiveth the word by the Spirit of truth receiveth it as it is preached by the Spirit of truth. . . . Wherefore, he that preacheth and he that receiveth, *understand one another, and both are edified and rejoice together."* (D&C 50:21–22; italics added.) When we listen with the Spirit, seeking to understand, spirit-to-spirit communication occurs, almost like an electric current flowing from one point to another. Barriers to understanding melt away.

72

True communication occurs. Trust is engendered as hearts open and tender emotions are brought to the surface. And, wonder of wonders, both persons involved are "edified and rejoice together."

In his book *The Seven Habits of Highly Effective People* (New York: Simon and Schuster, 1989), Stephen R. Covey teaches the skills involved in listening with the Spirit, which he terms "empathic listening." (See pp. 235–60.) A beginning step is to *play back the words the other person says*. For example, let's assume you are a stake president, and a bishop whom you are interviewing says, "I'm just so tired I can't go on. The company expects more and more from me. I just don't have time to be bishop." Essentially, all you have to do to start the process of listening with the Spirit is to repeat back what you've heard: "You're so tired you can't go on. You don't think you have time to be bishop any longer." Stopping there doesn't do much good, however, except to show that at least you're listening. Much more is needed if you are to really understand and communicate that understanding.

*Rephrasing the content* is the second stage. To the bishop's comment, "I'm just so tired I can't go on. The company expects more and more from me. I just don't have time to be bishop," the stake president might be tempted to say, "You're burned out, Bishop, and you want to be released." One of the problems with rephrasing, however, is that you may be tempted to make a judgment about the other person's situation, falling into the trap of prescribing before diagnosis is complete. What you say may be logical, or at least *seem* logical to you, but it may well be wrong and is highly likely to be incomplete at best. In this case it would be better to respond, "You are feeling pressured and are wondering how to fit everything in."

The third stage involves *reflecting feeling*, not logic. To the bishop's statement, the stake president might reply,

"You sound so frustrated, Bishop. Something must really be bothering you." This stage opens up feelings for examination. *Both feelings and logic* are reflected in stage four. The stake president's reply to the bishop's statement might be as follows: "You're really frustrated with the burdens of your calling and your job combined." Now you appeal both to feeling ("You're really frustrated") and to logic ("the burdens of your calling and your job combined"). Note that though the stake president seeks to understand, he retains his objectivity by not expressing sympathy for the bishop. Furthermore, in doing so, he helps the bishop look at his own problems with both emotion and logic. Only after you are certain you understand the other person should you begin to present your own position. Chances are your views may be different from those you started out with. Your own understanding may well have been altered by what you've learned. But at least there's now a basis for a meeting of minds.

## *"Come Now, and Let Us Reason Together"*

On the surface, Isaiah's persuasive invitation, "Come now, and let us reason together" (Isaiah 1:18) seems eminently sensible. After all, two rational people should be able to sit down together and reason out their differences, each giving a little if need be to arrive at a mutually acceptable position. Unfortunately, it's often not that easy, as illustrated by the following story.

A stake president did little to support the Boy Scouts in his stake. Whenever there was a Court of Honor to be held, he had an excuse for not being there. He was "too busy," or had an "unexpected crisis," or had some other unforeseen difficulty that prevented his attendance. He seemed reluctant to commit time, resources, and good people to the furtherance of Scouting in the stake. In fairness, it wasn't so much that he actively *opposed* Scouting as that he just didn't actively *support* it. Whatever the cause, there seemed more to the problem than met the eye. And so there was. To one whom he trusted, who knew how to listen with the Spirit, the stake president eventually confided his real reasons. "I was a Scout, a second-class Scout, when I was a boy," he said. "My folks were very poor, and I didn't even have a full uniform—just bits and pieces of patched and faded equipment. Whenever I went to Scouts, the other boys laughed at me. I've never forgotten the feelings of embarrassment and, yes, anger, that I felt. I guess that's why I still can't get enthusiastic about Scouts and Scouting." This stake president is an intensely private individual who finds it extremely hard to express the feelings of his heart. If he had been openly challenged, the truth would never have been revealed. He would, I believe, simply have drawn his dignity around him and refused to talk about the matter.

## The Many Facets of Truth

In our congregations we sometimes sing "Oh say, what is truth? 'Tis the fairest gem." (*Hymns,* no. 272.) Truth is indeed a jewel that sparkles with divine radiance, but it has many facets, many faces. I may see one face; you, another. Yet both may be right. Your point of view may be different from mine, but it deserves attention and respect. Even if I am right, you may not be wrong—only different.

Several years ago, a major international research foundation conducted a program to spray houses with pesticide to eliminate the mosquito vectors of yellow fever in a portion of the Amazon Basin. The first spraying episode went well; with the enthusiastic cooperation of the inhabitants, nearly every house in the three villages involved was sprayed. And the incidence of yellow fever dropped dramatically. When the spraying was repeated six months

75

later, only about two-thirds of the home-dwellers would let the spray team in to do its work. The others flatly refused. Six months after that, all doors were closed to the team, and machete-waving groups of householders refused to even let team members come into the villages. When pressed to explain their dramatic change in attitude, a spokesperson for the villagers had this to say: "As you know, nearly all of the men of these villages work in the local sugar factory. There are about 5,000 jobs and nearly 10,000 men. In the old days, before you started this spraying program, about half of the men would be sick at any given time. So, everyone who was well worked, and since everyone got sick periodically, all of the men worked part of the time. Now, thanks to your spraying program, there's no yellow fever around, and nearly everyone is physically well and able. But since there are only 5,000 jobs and 10,000 men, half of the men are permanently out of work, and their families are hungry. You can keep your pesticides; they don't help us!"

The physician who received that explanation told me of his reaction. "At first," he said, "I was dumfounded and more than a little irritated. Couldn't those simple peasants understand what we were doing for them? Didn't they know we were helping them? Talk about ingratitude!" Then he continued: "I began to cool off. I tried to understand where the villagers were coming from. I began to realize that from their point of view our activities, which had seemed so transparently good, even noble, to me, were to them a mixed blessing at best. I began to see how complex the situation really was and began to realize that preventing disease wasn't enough. *Real* help involved doing that, of course, but much more was required. We had to think of the need to provide jobs as well."

"The older I get," he concluded, "the more I realize there are no simple answers to complex human problems."

Each of us perceives the truth through the eyes of our own life experience, our own background. None of us can completely escape in mortality the conditioning of the environment in which we live. Each sees as "through a glass, darkly." (1 Corinthians 13:12.) The formative years of childhood and adolescence condition our thought patterns and perceptions more than we may care to admit. Because of this, some argue that truth is only relative and not absolute. The belief that there is no absolute truth lies at the root of the pernicious doctrine of situational ethics, with its seductive message that ethically appropriate behavior in one situation may not be morally correct in another. Such false teachings make God the author of confusion and demean humanity by neglecting our pre-earth life history and our possibilities as members of an eternal community to whom each of us owes responsibilities.

The many facets of truth can only be illuminated by Him who declared, "I am the light of the world: he that followeth me shall not walk in darkness, but shall have the light of life." (John 8:12.) That wonderful flood of light casts away the "cloud of darkness" from our minds and lights up our souls. (See Alma 19:6.) The eyes of our understanding are opened, and we see things as "they really are" and as "they really will be." (See Jacob 4:13.) We draw upon Christ's power to illuminate lives when we seek to listen with the Spirit.

As we listen with the Spirit, we come to appreciate that another's perception of the truth, while perhaps different from our own, is worthy of respect and, indeed, of admiration. Another's viewpoint may help us not only to better define and understand our own but perhaps to modify and adjust our own thinking, that "both [may be] edified and rejoice together." (D&C 50:22.)

## Perception Becomes Reality

In communicating with members of their flock and others, wise shepherds understand that even in situations where perception does not agree with the facts, it is perception, and not reality, that determines behavior. People act on what they believe to be true and may cling tightly to perceived notions that make no logical sense at all, even in the face of objective evidence to the contrary. Barriers in the mind, walls of fear and prejudice, may be the hardest to overcome. History abounds with examples.

For many years conventional wisdom held that the human body is physiologically incapable of running a mile in less than four minutes. Try as you may, proclaimed the athletes and their coaches, it just cannot be done. But a young Oxford University medical student, Roger Bannister, refused to believe what everyone else thought they knew. Bannister realized, from experience, that it was certainly possible to run one-quarter of a mile in a minute or less. Why then, he thought, couldn't a superbly trained runner run four sub-minute quarter miles back to back and break the four-minute barrier? Bannister trained hard and well, and on May 6, 1954, he put his theory to the test. So weary was he at the end of the run that after breaking the tape, Bannister collapsed into the arms of his supporters. An excited buzz went through the sedate English crowd. Was it possible Bannister had broken the four-minute mile? The knowledgeable ones among those present demurred: "Not possible, old chap. Can't be done, you know." Then came the announcement of Bannister's time: three minutes fifty-nine point four seconds. The impossible had been done! Bannister had proven that the barrier to the four-minute mile was psychological, not physiological. The limitation existed in the mind and not in the body.

Prince Henry the Navigator, the great fifteenth-century Portuguese patron of sea exploration, was the driving force behind intrepid seafarers whose tiny boats crept down the uncharted west coast of Africa, seeking for a sea route to the spices and jewels of India. It was a chilling experience for brave men who believed in their hearts that if they went too far southward into the Sea of Darkness, they would simply fall into a great void with "no race of men nor place of [habitation]." The rocky cliffs and swirling seas of the desolate coasts upon which they gazed seemed to their frightened minds to be the end of the world itself, the very gates of hell.

The place beyond which the seafarers dared not go was a tiny, almost imperceptible bump on the coastal outline of Africa just opposite the Canary Islands. Cape Bojadar ("bulging cape" in Portuguese), as it was called, was no more a barrier than dozens of others that Portuguese sailors had sailed serenely by in the past. But Bojadar became fixed in the minds of the Portuguese as the guardian of the gates of hell, beyond which they dared not pass. "These mariners of ours," wrote a contemporary of Prince Henry, "[were] threatened not only by fear but by its shadow." (Daniel Boorstin, *The Discoverers,* p. 166.) Over a ten-year period, Henry sent out no fewer than fifteen expeditions to push south beyond Cape Bojadar. Each failed, returning with one lame excuse or another to explain its inability to go where no one had gone before. The Cape was impassable, they proclaimed. Neither threat, flattery, nor bribes could change their minds. Finally, in 1434, yet another expedition was sent, with renewed promise of rewards for success. This time, the captain steered further out to sea, away from the crashing surf, before turning south. To his amazement, he found Bojadar already behind him and realized that he had neither dropped off the face of the earth nor sailed into the gates of hell. The barrier had been broken, and the shadow of fear erased.

## Strive Constantly for Clarity

Spirit-to-spirit communication is hard enough at the best of times, but when the message is garbled or ambiguous, the process becomes more difficult. For that reason, good communicators strive constantly for clarity. They work hard to make sure their message can't be taken two ways, recognizing that if the trumpet gives an uncertain sound, there may be unforeseen results. (See 1 Corinthians 14:8.) They ask others to "play back" the message to make sure it was received properly, and they edit and re-edit their written communications to ensure clarity.

Several years ago a friend of ours decided she would make hand-dipped chocolate candies as Christmas presents for family and friends. Since she'd had no previous experience in making chocolates, she called one of her Relief Society sisters on the telephone to get the recipe for the fondant. Then she started to work. For some unfathomable reason, she couldn't get the fondant to harden. She beat it, cooled it, added cornstarch in her desperation, and beat it again—all to no avail. Like some kind of primeval slime monster, the fondant oozed and slithered across the table and dripped onto the floor. Finally, frustrated and desperate, our friend flushed it all down the drain and collapsed, exhausted.

The next day, the would-be chocolate maker was discussing her lack of success with the woman who'd given her the recipe. "I just don't know what I did wrong," said she who had failed in her earnest attempt. "I just don't get it. I followed the recipe exactly: cream, icing sugar, and forty-five tablespoonsful of corn syrup, along with—" Her friend collapsed in laughter, exclaiming, "Forty-five tablespoonsful of corn syrup! I told you 'four to five,' not 'forty-five'!"

Clarity is particularly important on those occasions when the shepherd is required to "reprov[e] . . . with sharpness." Sharpness does not imply harshness or cruelty. To reprove with sharpness, as "moved upon by the Holy Ghost" involves teaching clearly, precisely, in ways that make a sharp distinction between error and truth and summon the individual to change and improve. As the scriptures point out (see D&C 121:43), reproof should not be undertaken without the assistance and approval of the Holy Ghost. Once done, reproof is to be followed promptly with an increase of love toward the one who was reproved, "lest he esteem thee to be his enemy." How critical it is under these circumstances that the one required to reprove say precisely what must be said but no more or less.

Historians agree that Brigham Young's magnificent leadership abilities were developed and polished during the struggles of the Saints across Iowa in 1846. It was a difficult time for "Brother Brigham" and for those who followed him. In the midst of the travail and turmoil, Hosea Stout recalled Brigham relating to the high council that in a dream he had seen Joseph sitting in a room. "Do you be sure and tell the brethren that it is all important for them to keep the spirit of the Lord," said Joseph. "Keep the quiet spirit of Jesus." (Eugene England, *Brother Brigham* [Salt Lake City: Bookcraft, 1980], p. 132.) To me, the instruction to "keep the quiet spirit of Jesus" says it all. What could be clearer! If shepherds are to communicate with the sheep of the flock in "the Lord's way," they must seek for the "quiet spirit of Jesus." It will teach and direct them, provide the power of discernment, and give assurance to both sheep and shepherd that they are on the Lord's errand. Then, and only then, will both be edified and rejoice together.

## Applying the Principles: Guidelines for Shepherds

Wise shepherds know the wisdom found in words attributed to Henry Ford: "If you think you can or think you can't, you're right." They know that the barriers to improved performance are more in the mind and heart than anything else, that human vision is blinded more by habit and fear than by reality. And so they carefully, lovingly, but persistently encourage and challenge, urging the flock to lift their eyes, to lengthen their stride, to get a vision of their real potential as sons and daughters of God. Wise shepherds set the example for their flocks. "Come, follow me," they say, asking no more of others than they give themselves. In the final analysis, it is the ability to develop a vision and then to communicate it to others in ways that first inspire and then transform that characterizes the great leader.

Wise shepherds, therefore, work hard to develop their own powers of communication, recognizing the ability of the written and spoken word to lift hearts and inspire noble deeds. Consider, for example, the majesty in these words Shakespeare has King Henry of England speak on the eve of the Battle of Agincourt (October 25, 1415). Henry's army seemed hopelessly outnumbered. The men were tired, cold, and hungry; their French opponents must surely sweep the field. But Henry raised the ardor and the fighting spirit of his men with these immortal words that "steel[ed his] soldiers' hearts":

> He, which hath no stomach to this fight,
> Let him depart, his passport shall be made,
> And crowns for convoy put into his purse;
> We would not die in that man's company,
> That fears his fellowship to die with us. . . .
> He that outlives this day, and comes safe home,
> Will stand a-tiptoe when this day is nam'd. . . .
> We few, we happy few, we band of brothers:
> For he today that sheds his blood with me
> Shall be my brother; be he ne'er so vile,
> This day shall gentle his condition:
> And gentlemen in England, now abed,

Shall think themselves accurs'd they were not here,
And hold their manhoods cheap, whiles any speaks
That fought with us upon Saint Crispin's day.
(*Henry V,* Act IV, scene iii.)

Wise shepherds strive mightily to improve their powers
to listen with the Spirit. They learn the skills involved but
recognize that ultimately success will lie not in skill but in
purity of heart and an "eye single to the glory of God."
(D&C 4:5.) Thus they strive to *really* listen, with all their
powers of concentration to blot out the vagrant, gypsy
thoughts that wander in and out of the mind and lead the
unwary away on flights of fancy. To learn to listen for the
still, small voice of the Spirit takes time and practice but,
above all else, a willingness to pay the price of hard work
and diligence.

I recall with pleasure stopping for a picnic lunch one
summer's day alongside a country road in Switzerland. It
was a scene of bucolic delight—the verdant mountain
meadows, trim Swiss farmsteads with their traditional ar-
chitecture and ubiquitous clusters of brown Swiss cattle.
I was especially thrilled to listen to the mellow ringing of
the cow bells. Each Swiss cow, I was told, has its own bell.
To me, all sounded alike, each note blending into a po-
lyphonic chorus with indistinguishable component parts.
But Swiss farmers learn to recognize the distinctive tone
of each individual bell amid all the others and can tell just
by listening which cows are with the herd and which are
missing. So, too, must the Lord's shepherds learn to listen
ever so carefully, to screen out extraneous noises and focus
on *the one,* to become a pure vessel through which and to
which the Spirit can be transmitted.

Wise shepherds know it is important to inspire others
by word and example. They recognize that people need a
vision of what they can do, of their true potential. Failing
that, they will in all likelihood remain satisfied with the

*status quo* and simply molder their lives away. "Where there is no vision, the people perish." (Proverbs 29:18.) The shepherds find the vision they are entrusted to impart in the holy scriptures and words of the living prophets and use them as a textbook to bring a knowledge of the glorious Christ and His gospel to the sheep. In the search for many-faceted truth, the shepherds are led by Him who proclaimed Himself to be the Light of the World. They read by that Light and not by the lamp of their own conceit.

Wise shepherds know that people can do great things if they catch the vision. They see beyond the glorious past to a future limited only by our ability to comprehend and then reach and stretch. With all of their might they attempt to communicate that vision, in clear and unmistakable ways.

# CHAPTER FOUR

# The Courageous Shepherd

Courage is one of the characteristics of effective shepherds. The need for courage in shepherds is constant. None can succeed without it. Shepherds are required to make decisions daily, often in the face of uncertainty and even of opposition. To make them wisely and righteously requires courage. Sometimes it will be the courage to say no that is needed; at other times, the courage to say yes. To listen to the whisperings of the Spirit and then to follow them in faith, even if the reasons for the Spirit-directed call to action are not yet clear, requires courage of a high order. Many times in the service of every shepherd, human wisdom simply does not suffice, and the courage of the day melts away in the dark night of uncertainty. Then, all one can do is turn to God and lean on Him, drawing from His divine strength. Such sentiments were found recorded on a scrap of paper in a slit-trench in Tunisia during the battle of El Agheila in World War II:

> Stay with me, God. The night is dark,
> The night is cold: My little spark
> Of courage dies. The night is long;
> Be with me, God, and make me strong.
> ("A Soldier—His Prayer," in John Bartlett, *Familiar Quotations*, 15th ed. [Boston: Little, Brown, and Company, 1980], p. 925.)

Courage wears many coats. It may be manifested in a single dramatic moment of conflict—in the clash and confusion of battle, for example—or in the less dramatic but perhaps even more noteworthy actions of moral courage that often go unnoticed and unsung.

Physical courage is lauded in every society, in every historical era. How thrilling it is to read of the exploits of great military champions and others who performed legendary feats of immense physical bravery, perhaps losing life or limb in the process. The annals of history are replete with stories of physical courage, an example of which is found in a battle that took place during the British-Zulu war in southern Africa in 1879.

Several thousand Zulu warriors fell upon the British garrison at Rorke's Drift, a plain but pleasant mission station located at a ford or drift across the Buffalo River. The station was defended by fewer than 140 British soldiers, of whom 36 were in hospital. They had only a few hours of warning about the impending attack. Frantically, they fortified their position, building a defensive wall of bags of corn and biscuit boxes. They had barely finished when the Zulus arrived, "thick as grass," as one observer recalled.

The Zulu warriors were an imposing spectacle of barbaric splendor. Those of one regiment carried black shields with white spots and wore vests of cowtails over their chests and backs. Others had red shields spotted with white; while those of a third regiment carried white shields and wore a white ostrich plume in their headdress. To a man they hurled themselves, time and again, in wave after wave, against the British wall.

Soon the ground was littered with dead and dying warriors, by the dozens and then by the hundreds. Those who reached the wall were bayoneted. Both sides fought with indescribable ferocity, often at close quarters, bayonet against stabbing spear. A thatch roof was set afire by the Zulus. In its light the battle raged on from 5:00 in the afternoon until after 2:00 A.M.

When the firing ended a few hours before dawn, the British defenders were exhausted, their shoulders bruised and swollen from the constant firing of their rifles, their faces blackened with gunpowder. Most of the defenders were wounded. Fifteen lay dead; two others were dying; ten more were severely wounded. The defenders collapsed over their rifles, totally spent. They could do no more. One more Zulu charge, at dawn, and all would be lost.

But as the sun appeared, the Zulus, instead of launching a final attack, rose from their resting spots, formed a column, and trotted off the field. They too had had enough.

The courage displayed on both sides was remarkable. Eleven Victoria Crosses for valor were awarded to the British defenders — the most in any single engagement in the history of the British army.

What happened at Rorke's Drift tells us much about human courage. Perhaps most important, it teaches the value of never giving up, of hanging on even in the face of overwhelming odds. Tenacity, an unwillingness to accept defeat, the bulldog determination to go on, on to victory or death, characterizes the best of human efforts. (See Donald R. Morris, *The Washing of the Spears* [London: Sphere Books, 1968], pp. 391–420, and Robert B. Edgerton, *Like Lions They Fought* [New York: Ballantine Books, 1988], pp. 96–107.)

Heroes come in all sizes and shapes and from every background imaginable; in most instances their actions could not have been predicted beforehand from previous behavior and are rooted in a mysterious amalgam of chemistry and circumstance.

There are important situational components to physical heroism. The presence of a charismatic leader can do wonders to transform demoralized, dispirited, frightened soldiers into raging lions. Writing of a critical point in a battle during the American Civil War, a young Confederate infantryman had this to say of General J.E.B. Stuart: "He leaped his horse over the breastworks near my company, and when he had reached a point about opposite the center of the brigade, while the men were loudly cheering him, he waved his hand toward the enemy and shouted, 'Forward, men! Forward! Just follow me! . . .' The men were wild with enthusiasm. . . . With courage and resolution, [they] poured over the breastworks after him like a wide raging torrent overcoming its barriers." The objective was seized and held. (Emory M. Thomas, *Bold Dragoon: The Life of J.E.B. Stuart* [New York: Harper and Row, 1986], pp. 211–12.)

The courage of the battlefield thrills and inspires all who witness or read of it. It inspires others to do their duty, to steel their hearts, to stand fast. Who could fail to be aroused by these words which Shakespeare's genius puts into the mouth of King Henry of England:

> Once more unto the breach, dear friends, once more;
> Or close the wall up with our English dead!
> In peace, there's nothing so becomes a man,
> As modest stillness and humility;
> But when the blast of war blows in our ears,
> Then imitate the action of the tiger:
> Stiffen the sinews, conjure up the blood,
> Disguise fair nature with hard-favored rage;
> Then lend the eye a terrible aspect.
> (*Henry V*, Act III, scene i.)

There is, however, another type of courage. It arises not from the sudden clash of combat or crisis that transcends rational thought but from the dogged determination to overcome fear, the willingness, in spite of terror, to carry out tasks that induce intense feelings of anxiety. Men and women who practice this form of courage are not likely to be those of whom songs are sung or for whom medals are struck. They are ordinary people who face their sometimes ordinary fears with dignity and courage, wrestle with them and subdue them, doing what must be done in spite of personal trepidation or dread. This form of courage is illustrated with power and clarity in the life and martyrdom of Joseph Standing.

The *Deseret News* for July 30, 1879, carried this ominous headline: "Another Martyr for the Truth." The accompanying story read in part as follows:

> Yesterday afternoon, Elder John Morgan, who has charge of the Southern States Mission, but who is at present staying in this city, received the following telegram:
>
> Catoosa Springs, Georgia, July 21, 3:50 p.m.
>
> John Morgan, Salt Lake:
>
> Jos. Standing, shot and killed today, near Varnell's, by a mob of ten or twelve men. Will leave with body for home, at once.
>
> Notify his family.
>
> Rudger Clawson

That terse announcement summarized an incident that shocked and outraged the Saints and underlined the opposition to the Latter-day Saint cause then being experienced in so many quarters. At the time of his death, Joseph Standing was a Mormon missionary, laboring in the rural counties of northern Georgia. It was a time of intense persecution of the Saints in Georgia and elsewhere in the South, much of it stirred up by local Protestant ministers. The Ku Klux Klan posted threatening notices and often rode at the mere appearance of the missionaries in a community. On two occasions in early 1879, mobs drove the elders from their fields of labor in Georgia; and on one such occasion, marauders entered the house of one of the local Saints, flourishing pistols and threatening to kill the inhabitants if they ever harbored the missionaries again.

By 1879, Joseph Standing had already completed one mission and was well into his second, having arrived in Georgia in February 1878. Born in Salt Lake City in October of 1854, he was noted for his "mild and gentle though firm disposition, one who would suffer wrong rather than do wrong." In May 1879, Joseph was set apart as president of the Georgia Conference of the Church.

Brother Standing had labored without a companion for several months until joined by Rudger Clawson in May of 1879. The two missionaries traveled on foot, without purse or scrip, depending on the kindness of those they met for food and lodging. In return, they helped with farm work and chores. They preached wherever they could, often in the homes of the faithful or in clearings in the woods.

Life was hard in rural Georgia after the Civil War. Wages averaged only twenty-five to fifty cents a day. Excessive taxes, including those on property, stifled personal initiative. Most people lived on cornbread and bacon. Many were dispirited and bitter. Yet most people were kind and hospitable to the missionaries. A trickle of honest seekers after truth, dissatisfied with sectarian preaching, began to join the Church. In August 1878 the total membership of the Southern States Mission was under 550 members; more than half that many had emigrated to the West in 1877.

Joseph Standing was by nature "mild and gentle," but he certainly did not lack for boldness and courage. Outraged by mob violence against the missionaries, he wrote a letter to the governor of Georgia seeking redress. "I am fully aware," Joseph wrote, "that the popular prejudice is very much against the Mormons. . . . But I also am aware that the laws of Georgia are strictly opposed to all lawlessness and extend to her citizens the right of worshipping

God according to the dictates of conscience . . . the laws, where prejudice exists, are not always executed with impartiality. A word or line from the governor would undoubtedly have the desired effect."

In response to Joseph's letter, a secretary to the governor replied that the state prosecuting attorney would be instructed to "inquire into the matter." Apparently, however, nothing further was done about the conditions mentioned in Joseph's letter.

A district conference was to be held in Rome, Georgia, in late July 1879. Elders Standing and Clawson, of course, planned to attend. They decided to stop for a few days at a little place called Varnell's Station and accompany the Saints there to conference. On the way, Joseph recounted to his companion the details of a deeply disturbing dream he'd recently had. In the dream, Joseph said, he had gone to Varnell's, "when suddenly clouds of intense blackness gathered overhead and all around me." In the dream he stopped at the home of a Mormon family and was told by the woman of the house, who was influenced "by a sense of great fearfulness," that he could not stay. Joseph awoke suddenly "without . . . being shown the end of trouble."

The dream deeply troubled Elder Standing. He was "fearful that something terrible was going to happen" and was filled with a sense of impending doom. Neither he nor Elder Clawson was able to interpret the dream. Despite their fears, the young men continued bravely on their journey.

The two young missionaries arrived at Varnell's Station late on the evening of Saturday, July 20, and made their way through the darkness to the home of a local member family. There Joseph's terrible dream began to be fulfilled. The woman of the house, in great agitation, told them they could not stay there. She warned the elders there was a "bitter and murderous" attitude toward them in the neighborhood. They spent a sleepless night at the home of a nonmember who promised to defend them so long as they were under his roof.

Joseph was frightened and anxious, with good reason. He had twice escaped a mob previously, when laboring with Elder John Morgan. He confided to Rudger "his intense horror of being whipped" and declared that "he would rather die than be subjected to such an indignity."

Despite his fears, however, Elder Standing evidently gave no thought to turning back. His deep conviction of the divinity of the cause in which he was engaged impelled him to go on. Neither fears of mob violence, a horror of whippings, nor the terrifying dream of blackness deterred him from his duty. How impressive is his moral courage!

The next morning, Sunday, July 21, the two missionaries resumed their journey. Suddenly, on a lonely, densely forested stretch of road, they were apprehended by a mob of twelve men, three on horseback, the rest on foot. The mobsters approached the missionaries with weapons drawn, cursing and shouting profanities. Joseph boldly spoke up: "By what authority do you arrest us upon the public highway here? If you have a warrant of arrest, we would like to see it."

"There is no law in Georgia for Mormons," was the reply.

The two missionaries were escorted down the road, threatened and bullied every step they took, and struck with clubs or guns if they did not move quickly enough. Certain they were being led to their deaths, they were told they would be whipped so they would never forget it. "You'll be pretty limber when we finish with you," one of their captors yelled.

What a horrifying experience that must have been for those two brave young souls, particularly for Joseph, who undoubtedly sensed the fulfillment of his horrible dream of darkness.

At first, it appears the mob intended only to beat the missionaries and put them on a train out of the state. "If we ever find you in this part of the country we will hang you by the neck like dogs," the leader of the group snarled.

The mob and their captives stopped by a secluded stream of clear water about fifty yards off the road. Three of the mobsters left, to reconnoiter the road ahead. Those who remained continued to threaten and bully the elders. Finally, the three who had left returned. "Follow us," they ordered. Elder Standing, undoubtedly with thoughts of torture and death in his mind, made some resistance. As quick as thought, one of the mob shot him dead. The leader of the mob then pointed to Elder Clawson. "Shoot that man," he ordered his fellow ruffians. Elder Clawson, certain he, too, would die, collected himself, folded his arms calmly, and said, "Shoot." Someone yelled, "Don't shoot." The guns were lowered, and the immediate danger passed. Clawson was allowed to leave. As soon as he could make his way to a telegraph, he wired John Morgan in Utah and informed the governor of Georgia, whose failure to respond positively to Elder Standing's earlier letter could not go unnoticed.

When Brother Clawson arrived back at Varnell's Station, he found that the body of Joseph Standing had been mutilated by his murderers. The Coroner's Jury found that "twenty shots or more from guns or pistols" had penetrated Joseph's body.

The body of Joseph Standing was taken back to Utah by Elder Clawson and buried on August 3. Elders John Taylor and George Q. Cannon spoke at the funeral.

Three of the killers were tried by the State of Georgia for their crime—in a trial that John Morgan described as "a farce." The prosecuting attorney was quoted by elders

Morgan and Clawson as saying before the trial, "It will be impossible to reach conviction on account of the prejudice of the people." Not surprisingly, all defendants were acquitted of all charges.

In 1952, President David O. McKay dedicated a small memorial park honoring Joseph Standing, on the site of his murder. The land had been donated to the Church by a local resident.

Time has faded remembrances of the circumstances of Joseph Standing's martyrdom. The great physical and moral courage he exhibited, however, stands forever as a shining example to all who cherish religious freedom. (See *Deseret News*, July 30 and August 1, 1879; David S. Hoopes and Roy Hoopes, *The Making of a Mormon Apostle, the Story of Rudger Clawson* [New York: Madison Books, 1990], pp. 13–31; Ken Driggs, " 'There Is No Law in Georgia for Mormons': The Joseph Standing Murder Case of 1879," *Georgia Law Quarterly*, 73:745–72.)

Without belittling the courage of combat, the bravery of that single dramatic moment, the moral courage exhibited by Joseph Standing is even more noble and hence more to be applauded. Moral courage comes from cool heads and thinking minds rather than those ablaze with the danger and stress of a moment of crisis or combat. It involves the rational weighing of alternatives while knowing full well that one of the options available is fraught with danger. Acceptance of that superficially less-attractive alternative may lead to persecution, criticism, dismissal. It may even lead to death itself. Yet that is the chosen, lonely path. It alone is the way of honor and integrity, demanded by the conscience in full knowledge of the likely consequences. To choose another way would certainly be easier. Instead of obloquy, abuse, or persecution, there would be applause, the favors of prominent people, acclaim, or material gain. But the "easy way out" represents the path of dishonor and is simply not acceptable, whatever the cost, because it violates a sense of moral integrity and sacrifices that which is most dear on the altar of expediency.

How noble are those who exhibit the moral courage to live by their adherence to a higher order of truth, whose souls will not be tarnished by the easy accommodation of an elastic conscience to a wicked and perverse world, who cannot live save by clinging to principle. To such celestial souls the conscience—devoid of offense toward God or man (see Acts 24:16)—serves as a guide or guardian. Winston Churchill spoke of such: "The only guide to a man is his conscience; the only shield to his memory is the rectitude and sincerity of his actions. It is very imprudent to walk through life without this shield, because we are so often mocked by the failure of our hopes and the upsetting of our calculations; but with this shield, however the fates may play, we march always in the ranks of honor." (In *Familiar Quotations,* p. 744.)

Many men and women of conscience throughout history have set great examples of moral courage. One such was John Fisher, Bishop of Rochester, England, whose conscience forbade his acceptance of the doctrine of Royal Supremacy over that of the church and would not permit him to agree that Henry VIII's divorce from Catherine of Aragon was valid. (In recounting Fisher's story, I hasten to add that although Fisher was a good and gentle man, he lacked an understanding of the fullness of the gospel, which was not restored to earth until nearly three centuries after his death. One need not fully approve of Fisher's theology to applaud his courage.)

Fisher was confined to the Tower of London under conditions of extreme deprivation. He was denied clothing to keep him warm and decent food; his piteous entreaties for humane treatment were dismissed by the king's lackeys as "mere craft and cunning." On June 17, 1535, Fisher was pronounced guilty of treason and sentenced to a traitor's death by beheading.

Early in the morning of the day he was to die, Fisher dressed in the clean, warm clothing he had at last received. Then he placed a fur cape over his shoulders to keep warm. "Oh, my Lord," exclaimed his jailer, "what need you be so careful of your health at this time?" Fisher, old and sick, did not want to shiver lest the people think him afraid.

As he neared the scaffold, Fisher opened his Bible. "Oh, Lord," he said, "this is the last time that I shall ever open this book, let some comfortable place now chance to me, whereby I, Thy poor servant, may glorify Thee in this my last hour." The book fell open at this passage from John 17:4–5: "I have glorified thee on the earth: I have finished the work which thou gavest me to do. And now, O Father, glorify thou me with thine own self."

"Here," said the pious old man, "is learning enough for me to my life's end." To the executioner he proclaimed, "I forgive thee with all my heart, and I trust thou shalt see me overcome this storm with courage." His head was severed with a single blow of the axe.

Two weeks later, Fisher's friend, Sir Thomas More, followed him to the scaffold. Like Fisher, More refused to take the oath of supremacy, giving precedence to king over church. He, too, died true to conscience and conviction. (See Christopher Hibbert, *Tower of London* [New York: Newsweek Book Division, 1971], pp. 50–52.)

The scriptures are replete with examples of men and women of great moral courage, including Joseph, who withstood attempted seduction by Potiphar's wife (Genesis 39:7–21); Esther, the Jewish maiden who risked her life to save her people (Esther 1–10); Daniel, who was cast into a den of lions for his refusal to worship false gods (Daniel 6); the three young Israelites cast into a fiery furnace because they refused to worship an idol (Daniel 3); Abinadi, who gave his life rather than deny the truth (Mosiah 11–17); and the great Nephi, who endured the obloquy and bitter enmity of his brethren (1 Nephi 17–18).

Who has not thrilled at Luke's account of the courage of Peter and John? Brought before the council for having healed a man "lame from his mother's womb," the two apostles were asked: "By what power, or by what name, have ye done this?" Peter replied in these words of simple majesty:

> Ye rulers of the people, and elders of Israel, If we this day be examined of the good deed done to the impotent man, by what means he is made whole; Be it known unto you all, and to all the people of Israel, that by the name of Jesus Christ of Nazareth, whom ye crucified, whom God raised from the dead, even by him doth this man stand here before you whole. This is the stone which was set at nought of you builders, which is become the head of the corner. Neither is there salvation in any other: for there is none other name under heaven given among men, whereby we must be saved. (Acts 4:8–12.)

The council members were nonplussed, not knowing how to deal with the two mighty men of God. "What shall we do to these men?" they asked.

> For that indeed a notable miracle hath been done by them is manifest to all them that dwell in Jerusalem; and we cannot deny it. But that it spread no further among the people, let us straitly threaten them, that they speak henceforth to no man in this name. And they called them, and commanded them not to speak at all nor teach in the name of Jesus. But Peter and John answered and said unto them, Whether it be right in the sight of God to hearken unto you more than unto God, judge ye. For we cannot but speak the things which we have seen and heard. (Acts 4:16–20.)

What magnificent moral courage!

The moral courage of the Prophet Joseph Smith was exhibited numerous times during his life. When, as a pure-hearted boy who had seen a vision he attempted to speak of it to a sectarian preacher, he was severely rebuked. In the Prophet's words:

> I was greatly surprised at his [the preacher's] behavior; he treated my communication not only lightly, but with great contempt. . . . I soon found . . . that my telling the story had excited a great deal of prejudice against me among professors of religion, and was the cause of great persecution, which continued to increase; and though I was an obscure boy . . . men of high standing would take notice sufficient to excite the public mind against me, and create a bitter persecution; and this was common among all the sects — all united to persecute me. (JS–H 1:21–22.)

Joseph, however, could not be silent, though the persecution he endured was "the cause of great sorrow" to him. Wrote he:

> I had actually seen a light, and in the midst of that light I saw two Personages, and they did in reality speak to me; and though I was hated and persecuted for saying that I had seen a vision, yet it was true; and while they were persecuting me, reviling me, and speaking all manner of evil against me falsely for so saying, I was led to say in my heart: Why persecute me for telling the truth? I have actually seen a vision; and who am I that I can withstand God, or why does the world think to make me deny what I have actually seen? For I had seen a vision; I knew it, and I knew that God knew it, and I could not deny it, neither dared I do it; at least I knew that by so doing I would offend God, and come under condemnation. I had now got my mind satisfied so far as the sectarian world

was concerned—that it was not my duty to join with any of them, but to continue as I was until further directed. (JS–H 1:25–26.)

From those early stirrings of persecution until his martyrdom more than two decades later, Joseph knew no peace. At a particularly dispiriting time in his life, while he and several companions languished in the jail at Liberty, Missouri, in March 1839, the Lord reminded His prophet-son of Joseph's lot in life and the eternal reward that would be his:

> The ends of the earth shall inquire after thy name, and fools shall have thee in derision, and hell shall rage against thee; while the pure in heart, and the wise, and the noble, and the virtuous, shall seek counsel, and authority, and blessings constantly from under thy hand. And thy people shall never be turned against thee by the testimony of traitors. . . . Hold on thy way, and the priesthood shall remain with thee. . . . Thy days are known, and thy years shall not be numbered less; therefore, fear not what man can do, for God shall be with you forever and ever. (D&C 122:1–3, 9.)

The demands of moral courage may require one to give up cherished ideas, to abandon old ways and old friends, perhaps to accept ridicule, opposition, persecution, and abuse. Consider Serge Baliff, for example, a preacher whose pulpit was that of the great cathedral in Lausanne, Switzerland. He was respected, looked up to, a man of substance and influence. But one day in the early 1850s two young men from America came to his door, preaching of a new revelation from on high. The gospel of Christ in all its power and purity had again been restored to the earth, they said. The heavens were opened, the authority of the priesthood of God, which they bore, had been given again to man. They spoke of a young prophet—of his vision of the Father and the Son, and they urged Serge Baliff to listen. He did, was converted, joined The Church of Jesus Christ of Latter-day Saints, and was promptly dismissed from his ecclesiastical duties, rejected by friends and associates, jostled and hectored on the streets, and snubbed by Swiss society. But Brother Ballif knew that his testimony was true; armed with that power, he preached the restored gospel against great opposition. In 1854 he left his native land and led a party of several hundred Swiss Saints to America. His great-grandson, President Ezra Taft Benson, serves the Church today as Prophet, Seer, and Revelator.

I was privileged to hear President Benson tell that story at the organization of the Geneva Switzerland Stake in June of 1982. His voice cracking with emotion, Elder Benson bore a powerful testimony that faithful Saints from earlier times were present in the hall that day—and great was their joy to see a landmark achievement of progress they had helped start.

The life of Alma the younger is a great example of the moral courage involved in repentance. For many years Alma traveled the dark, well-trodden highway of sin, rebellion, and destruction. The Nephite record is silent on the details of the sins of Alma but indicate that he was a "very wicked and an idolatrous man, . . . a man of many words, [who] did speak much flattery to the people; therefore he led many of the people to do after the manner of his iniquities. And he became a great hinderment to the prosperity of the church of God." (Mosiah 27:8–9.)

Significantly, the damage Alma did was not limited to his personal influence. Perhaps greater harm came about because he gave "a chance for the enemy of God to exercise his power [over the people]." (Mosiah 27:9.) That power, which leads the unwary "carefully down to hell" (2 Nephi 28:21) often is both seductive and cumulative. C. S. Lewis described how the devil works in the famous *Screwtape Letters*—a fictional account of instructions given by an old, experienced devil, Screwtape, to his uncertain apprentice, Wormwood:

> You will say that these are very small sins; and doubtless, like all young tempters, you are anxious to be able to report spectacular wickedness. . . . It does not matter how small the sins are, provided that their cumulative effect is to edge the man away from the Light and out into the Nothing. . . . Indeed, the safest road to Hell is the gradual one — the gentle slope, soft underfoot, without sudden turnings, without milestones, without signposts. (*The Screwtape Letters* [Glasgow: William Collins Sons and Co., 1987], pp. 64–65.)

And so Alma went about, doing the devil's work, denying all that his prophet-father taught and stood for, rebelling against God and seeking to destroy the Church. Finally, one day, God took a hand in Alma's life. The prayers of the people and of Alma's father had been heard. (Mosiah 27:14.) An angel appeared to Alma and his companions and spoke to them, as it were, with a voice of thunder. To Alma he said, "If thou wilt of thyself be destroyed, seek no more to destroy the church of God." (Alma 36:9.) Alma was struck dumb by this encounter with the heavenly messenger and for three days and three nights was unable to speak or stand.

With great moral courage, Alma began a process of serious self-examination, perhaps for the first time. Knowledge of the shabby selfishness of his life racked his soul with "inexpressible horror," and he was "tormented with the pains of hell." (Alma 36:14–15.) Alma recalled having heard his father "prophesy unto the people concerning the coming of one Jesus Christ, a Son of God, to atone for the sins of the world." (Alma 36:17.) He had the courage to accept Christ, to leave behind his previous life, and to commit himself to a "mighty change." As he cried out in terrible anguish, "O Jesus, thou Son of God, have mercy on me" (Alma 36:18), a great beam of celestial light and peace fell, as it were, on Alma's heart, replacing pain with an effulgent joy as exquisite and sweet as his pain had been bitter and galling. He could remember his pains no more; his sins no longer harrowed up his soul. He had been "born of God, and [was] filled with the Holy Ghost." (Alma 36:24.)

That is what true repentance born of moral courage does—it cleanses and heals and purifies. It changes hearts, turning them from sin to a desire to do good. Wickedness loses its allure and is seen in its true light as a shabby counterfeit of happiness. Alma, who had scorned, ridiculed, and mocked sacred things now wished—nay, longed—to be with the God whom he loved. He began to testify of the goodness of God to him. So full was his joy that he could not be silent: "O that I were an angel, and could have the wish of mine heart, that I might go forth and speak with the trump of God, with a voice to shake the earth, and cry repentance unto every people!" (Alma 29:1.) And, in common with all penitent, repentant, courageous souls, Alma changed the way he lived, trying to make up for his errors, to start a new life and render restitution. "From that time even until now," he declared, "I have labored without ceasing, that I might bring souls unto repentance; that I might bring them to taste of the exceeding joy of which I did taste." (Alma 36:24.)

Doubt and disbelief had been displaced by the calm certainty of true faith; rancor and rebellion gave way to rapturous affirmation of divine support. Alma said the Lord had supported him "under trials and troubles of every kind, yea, and in all manner of afflictions. . . . I do put my trust in him, and he will still deliver me." (Alma 36:27.) That last phrase, "He will still deliver me," speaks volumes about Alma's deep sense of wonderment that he, who had been such a great sinner, was still counted worthy of saving—that God's love and redemptive power could penetrate even into the depths of Alma's wayward world. But Alma, and each of us, has that promise: "Though [our] sins be as scarlet, they shall be as white as snow; though they be red like crimson, they shall be as wool." (Isaiah 1:18.)

It took great moral courage for Alma to accept the pain and suffering of his repentance. Indeed repentance *always* involves suffering. There is no other way it can be accomplished. Leaving behind addictive habits, carnal pleasures, or associates who degrade rather than exalt may indeed cause pain in the short run. The process involved is analogous to that used in the surgical treatment of an infected wound. In treating such a wound, the surgeon first removes dead and infected tissue. He scrubs and cleanses. Only then can the healing process begin. So it is with our spiritual wounds: we must be cleansed and purified before our souls can heal. But before the healing process can start, we must have the moral courage to recognize the need for change, accept the bitterness of remorse, resolve to change, and then move from the pain of sin to the peace of salvation and exaltation.

The physical courage of the early pioneer members of The Church of Jesus Christ of Latter-day Saints is justly renowned. But we must never forget the great moral courage it took to join the Church in pioneer times, knowing that rejection, persecution, abuse, and exile would almost inevitably result. Consider this experience of Priscilla Mogridge Stains, an Englishwoman born in 1823, who emigrated to America after her conversion. Her own words tell best the trials that lay ahead of her as she moved to embrace the restored gospel:

> It was a great trial for a young maiden (I was only nineteen years of age) to forsake all for the

103

gospel—father, mother, brothers and sisters—and to leave my childhood's home and native land, never expecting to see it again. This was the prospect before me. The Saints were already leaving the fatherland, in obedience to the doctrine of gathering, which was preached at this time with great plainness by the elders as an imperative command of God. We looked upon the gathering as necessary to our salvation. Nothing of our duty in this respect was concealed, and we were called upon to emigrate to America as soon as the way should open, to share the fate of the Saints, whatever might come. Young as I was and alone of all my family in the faith, I was called to take up my cross and lay my earthly all upon the altar; yet so well satisfied was I with my new religion that I was willing to make every sacrifice for it in order to gain my salvation and prove myself not unworthy of the Saints' reward.

Having determined to be baptized, I resolved to at once obey the gospel, although it was midwinter and the weather bitterly cold.

It is proper to here state that baptism was a trial to the converts in England in those days. They had to steal away, even unknown to their friends oftentimes, and scarcely daring to tell the Saints themselves that they were about to take up the cross; and not until the ordinance had been administered, and the Holy Ghost gave them boldness, could they bring themselves to proclaim openly that they had cast in their lot with the despised Mormons. Nor was this all, for generally the elders had to administer baptism when the village was wrapt in sleep, lest persecutors should gather a mob to disturb the solemn scene with gibes and curses, accompanied with stones or clods of earth torn from the river bank and hurled at the disciple and minister during the performance of the ceremony.

On the evening of a bitterly cold day in midwinter, as before stated, I walked four miles to the house of a local elder for baptism. Arriving at his house, we waited until midnight, in order that the neighbors might not disturb us, and then repaired to a stream of water a quarter of a mile away. Here we found the water, as we anticipated, frozen over, and the elder had to chop a hole in the ice large enough for the purpose of baptism. It was a scene and an occasion I shall never forget. Memory today brings back the emotions and sweet awe of that moment. None but God and his angels, and the few witnesses who stood on the bank with us, heard my covenant; but in the solemnity of that midnight hour it seemed as though all nature were listening, and the recording angel writing our words in the book of the Lord. . . . Is it strange that such a scene, occurring in the life of a Latter-day Saint, should make an everlasting impression, as this did on mine?

Having been thus baptized, I returned to the house in my wet and freezing garments. (In *Remarkable Stories from the Lives of Latter-day Saint Women*, compiled by Leon R. Hartshorn [Salt Lake City: Deseret Book Co., 1976], pp. 234–36.)

Anna Gaarden Widtsoe, whose gifted son John Andreas Widtsoe became a member of the Quorum of the Twelve Apostles, had a similar trying introduction to the gospel. She first heard of it from a humble shoemaker, Olaus Johnsen, who stuffed gospel tracts into the toes of her children's shoes which she had given him to repair. To her confused query, "Who are you?" he replied with simple dignity, "I am a member of the Church of Christ — we are called Mormons. We have the truth of God."

Mormons! She recoiled in dismay. Her minister had warned her about the Mormons! She had innocently become involved with a dangerous group of people! She hurriedly left the shoemaker's shop, anxious to be away from heresy. Yet she could not forget what Brother Johnsen had said, nor the sincerity of his humble message and testimony. Might it be that the Mormons, of whom she had heard nothing but bad, could have the truth of God? No, the very thought was absurd! Yet—

The seeds of doubt, and then of hope, began to spring up in her bosom. So began two years of struggle for Anna Widtsoe's soul. Slowly she began to understand that she was in the presence of eternal truths, that she had found a pearl of great price. She fought against the needed change but at length admitted she had found the truth and could not deny it.

Mormon meetings were held on the second floor of the shoemaker's humble log home. Anna was at first appalled by the primitive meeting conditions and dismayed by the humble status of the Church members. The Norway of her day had sharp class distinctions; as a member of the professional class, she at first had great difficulty in accepting humble working folk as brothers and sisters. Yet so courageous was she that one day, several months later, as the truth was becoming clear to her, she came home after the Sunday meeting and said aloud to herself, "Must I step down to that? Yes, if it is the truth I must do so."

On April 1, 1881, a little more than two years after she first heard the gospel, Anna was baptized in the icy water of Trondhjem fjord. Within the year, she and her two sons left for America. (See John A. Widtsoe, *In the Gospel Net: The Story of Anna A. G. Widtsoe* [Independence, Mo.: Zions Printing and Publishing Co., 1941], pp. 53–57.)

Thank God for the life and example of such a noble, courageous soul!

It is thrilling to observe the lives of the humble members of the Church who exhibit such remarkable moral courage and integrity. Several years ago, I sat in the temple at Zollikofen, near Berne, Switzerland, with a French brother from the Nice France Stake. He had traveled fourteen hours, sitting up in the train, to come to the Lord's House, slept in the Church hostel with eleven other men in a room with four rows of triple bunk beds, risen at five A.M. so he could get a place at the first session, and then tenderly and lovingly helped a crippled and blind brother throughout the day. As I shook his rough workman's hand and looked at his weatherbeaten face, it was plain to see he was of humble circumstances. But I thought to myself: "God bless you, my faithful brother, to whom the gospel means so much. God bless you for your courage, your willingness to sacrifice, and your loving spirit."

Susan McCarty, a young married woman then nineteen years old, first heard the message of the Restoration in 1909 from missionaries laboring in the neighborhood of her home in the little rural community of Turkey Creek, Louisiana. Displaying great courage, Susan soon joined The Church of Jesus Christ of Latter-day Saints, as did her brother, Hardy Clark. Susan's husband did not join though he promised to protect and support her in her actions. Given the attitudes held by many people in the southern states toward the Latter-day Saints in those days, that offer of protection and support was deeply appreciated. For more than four decades (until 1956 when a Church-owned building was constructed), members of the Turkey Creek Branch met on Sundays at Susan's home or that of her brother, Hardy Clark. Only occasionally were there more than twenty or twenty-five in attendance.

The meetings were simple. The little group prayed and sang together, and Brother Clark, who was the presiding elder, blessed the sacrament. The hymns were sung without accompaniment; hymn books became available only in the 1940s. Every week one of the members talked for a few minutes about one of the basic principles of the Gospel. Simple classes for adults, teenagers, and children were held. Testimony meeting was held once a month. Usually all of those present who were old enough to speak for themselves gave a humble but strong testimony.

After the meetings were over, the people lingered to talk to each other, and sometimes there was a "dinner on the ground." There were occasional visits from traveling missionaries or others from Church headquarters, but such contact was infrequent, especially in the early years.

The scriptures played a major role in the lives of those humble Saints. They had a strict habit of daily scripture study, with emphasis on the Book of Mormon. The scriptures were talked about around the dinner table each day, and family members read together from them each evening. Faith and trust in the promises of the Lord were the bedrock principles from which these humble Saints operated.

From that simple home-centered branch of the Church in Turkey Creek have come at least twelve full-time missionaries; two patriarchs; and a stake president, Ruben B. Clark, president of the Denham Springs Louisiana Stake, from whom much of the information presented about his family was obtained (in a letter to the author, 5 January 1991). Susan died in January 1991, in her hundredth year. As she lay dying, she gathered around her the many members of her family and bore fervent testimony of the truthfulness of the gospel. I look forward to meeting her in the hereafter and salute her and the other humble Saints in Turkey Creek as courageous, modern-day pioneers.

### Applying the Principles, Guidelines for Shepherds

The importance of courage in shepherds cannot be overemphasized. It is an essential ingredient for success. No shepherd—not bishops, stake presidents, or other priesthood and sister leaders—can succeed without courage. Actions that characterize courageous shepherds include the following:

1. *Shepherds must be dedicated to the principles of the restored gospel and resolutely refuse to weaken them or negotiate them away, regardless of pressure or circumstances.* Those principles are nonnegotiable, independent of culture or historical period. They are the foundation upon which all true leaders must stand.

Successful leadership in the Church—indeed, in life itself—must be centered on the principles of the restored gospel and absolute integrity to them. Adherence to anything else, including the multitude of personality centered techniques and skills so avidly presented as "quick fixes" in much of the popular "success" literature, produces little of lasting worth. Such leadership fads come and go, their promises of easy success never fulfilled. At best they are of marginal value; at worst, a malignant distortion of truth that destroys the person addicted to them.

In its essence, therefore, leadership is about character, about values such as courage that never change, though they may not be popular. Stephen R. Covey has developed this theme with power in his books *Seven Habits of Highly Effective People* and *Principle-Centered Leadership.* Such values deserve to be pondered and applied in our lives.

Devotion to the foundational principles of the gospel is possible only if shepherds clearly understand the nature and content thereof. Shepherds must, therefore, be dedicated students of the scriptures and the words of the living prophets. They must strive and struggle for knowledge and understanding. Prayer, pleading, importuning, and plenty of plain hard work are involved. No shortcuts are available; the price must be paid. Steadfast courage is required.

2. *Courageous shepherds are not afraid to lift up their voices, as with the sound of a trump (see D&C 29:4) to proclaim the truths of the restored gospel.* Unconstrained by a "fear of man" (D&C 60:2), they are quick to take every honorable op-

portunity to proclaim and defend the truth. They act, however, with wisdom and prudence, taking care not to revile against the revilers (see D&C 19:30), turning the other cheek (see Matthew 5:39), and trusting in God to do as He will with those who persecute the faithful.

3. *Courageous shepherds practice "tough love" with those for whom they bear responsibility,* knowing that even the best require correction and reproof if spiritual growth and development are to continue. As Elder Stephen L Richards said: "It is a kindness to reprove in the spirit of love. It is an unkindness to mitigate the gravity of offenses in those for whose guidance and direction we have responsibility." (*Conference Report,* April 1957, p. 97.)

Even the incomparable Joseph the Prophet was corrected on numerous occasions by his tutoring Lord. (See, for example, D&C 10:1–3.) Courageous leaders who understand that "an ounce of prevention is worth a pound of cure" recognize that for maximum effectiveness reproof must be done "betimes" — that is, early on, before undesirable ways and habits get too firmly entrenched. They recognize also that reproof must be linked with an increased demonstration of love, lest he who has been reproved "esteem thee to be his enemy." (D&C 121:43.) Indeed, the motivation for reproof must be love unfeigned rather than the too-common desire to exercise power, "pull rank," or gratify ego. President Joseph F. Smith expressed these thoughts:

> If there are any of my friends who can show me where I fail, oh come to me like a brother, not fault-finding, but come to me as a savior upon Mount Zion and show me my error and give me a chance by the aid of your counsel and advice to me to overcome the evil you see in me, whether you see it literally or whether you simply imagine it. Let me learn to do right by your help. Don't crush me down. Don't discard me. Don't throw me over into

the scrap pile because you think I am not as perfect as I ought to be. Rather be patient with my imperfections, and try to help me overcome them and to live nearer unto the Lord than ever before. That is the part of a savior upon Mount Zion. I am talking to the priesthood and to the Latter-day Saints, and to those that preside in the Church, and to those that exercise authority in the midst of the people. (*Conference Report*, April 1913, p. 8.)

I recall with deep gratitude an example of "tough love" that I was too immature at the time to appreciate properly. Many years ago when I was in high school in Western Canada, one of my teachers was Miss Marjorie Knapp. She was single, somewhat staid in her habits and old-fashioned in her dress. Sad to say, she was the object of considerable adolescent banter and ridicule. But Miss Knapp was a very good teacher and a fine person who expected a lot from her students.

Like many other teenaged boys, I was drifting along, doing no more than was necessary to get by with mediocre grades and trying to be "cool" by affecting an unconcern about most things, particularly academic excellence. One day Miss Knapp returned an exam paper marked with the magnificent grade of C+ and a penciled notation: "See me after class." I did so, a little resentful at being singled out and less than gratified with the grade awarded. Miss Knapp looked at me over her heavy spectacles. "You have a lot of unused ability," she said, "and the potential to go on to do much university work. You can do better than a C+; why don't you decide to do so?"

That conversation, which I didn't appreciate at the time, was a critical change-point for me. On reflection, I decided that maybe working more *was* a good idea, and my grades began to improve. So, too, did my attitude. Several years later, after passing a graduate language requirement, I wrote to Miss Knapp, who was by that time in a nursing home, telling her how grateful I was she had loved me enough to challenge me. I'm told she appreciated the letter. I know I enjoyed sending it.

Shepherds may lack the courage to practice "tough love" because they are afraid of hurting the feelings of the person being corrected or reproved. In a way, such attitudes are admirable; no leader in Christ's Church should ever want to hurt another human soul. But when godly chastisement is required to save a soul, the shepherd who is afraid to do what must be done is untrue to the trust reposed in him or her by the Lord and His servants. President Brigham Young's wise counsel should guide shepherds required to correct those in their charge:

> If you are ever called upon to chasten a person, never chasten beyond the balm you have within you to bind up. I might call some of you to witness that I chasten you, but there is not a soul that I chasten but what I feel as though I could take them and put them in my bosom and carry them with me day by day. They deserve chastisement, but God forbid that I should chasten beyond the healing balm I have to save them and make better men of them. . . . I want to know how to lead you with that intelligence to enable you to live to an everlasting life, that you may be saved in the kingdom of God. I say again, Do not chasten beyond the balm you have within you. If you have the saving influence within you, it is well. When you have the chastening rod in your hands, ask God to give you wisdom to use it, that you may not use it to the destruction of an individual, but to his salvation. (*Journal of Discourses,* 9:124–25.)

Shepherds who "dish out" tough love must be prepared to "take it" as well. To do so requires substantial courage. Sad to say, the history of the Church is littered with the wreckage of the lives of men and women whose pride prevented them from accepting correction. Men such as Thomas B. Marsh lacked sufficient internal security to be open to correction and felt so threatened by godly chastisement they could not accept it.

Courageous shepherds, on the other hand, recognize that even the best require correction. They have in mind the example of the Prophet Joseph Smith, who required chastening by a loving Master despite his great spiritual gifts. They understand that honest feedback is essential for progress. Because they are committed to continual learning, they recognize that others can teach them much. Courageous shepherds seek counsel and advice; they are not offended by honest, empathetic correction or reproof. They accept it, make the necessary changes, and go on.

President Gordon B. Hinckley tells how he was deeply discouraged by the environment and circumstances in which he found himself during the first few weeks of his missionary service in England. Of those troubled times he has written:

> I was not well when I arrived. Those first few weeks, because of illness and the opposition which we felt, I was discouraged. I wrote a letter home to my good father and said that I felt I was wasting my time and his money. He was my father and my stake president, and he was a wise and inspired man. He wrote a very short letter to me which said, "Dear Gordon, I have your recent letter. I have only one suggestion, forget yourself and go to work." Earlier that morning in our scripture class my companion and I had read these words of the Lord: "Whosoever will save his life shall lose it; but whosoever shall lose his life for my sake and the gospel's, the same shall save it." (Mark 8:35.)
>
> Those words of the Master, followed by my father's letter with his counsel to forget myself and go to work, went into my very being. With my father's letter in hand, I went into our bedroom in the house at 15 Wadham Road, where we lived,

and got on my knees and made a pledge with the Lord. I covenanted that I would try to forget myself and lose myself in his service.

That July day in 1933 was my day of decision. I do not say it egotistically. I say it humbly and with gratitude. A new light came into my life and a new joy into my heart. The fog of England seemed to lift, and I saw the sunlight. I had a rich and wonderful mission experience, for which I shall ever be grateful, laboring in Preston where the work began and in other places where it had moved forward, including the great city of London, where I served the larger part of my mission. (*BYU Studies,* 27 [Spring 1987]: 10.)

It is safe to say that President Hinckley would not be where he is today, a member of The First Presidency of The Church of Jesus Christ of Latter-day Saints, had he not been reproved and challenged to do better at a critical time in his life. Thank God for a father who loved his son enough to correct him, and for a son who had the courage to accept the correction in the spirit in which it was given and resolve to do better!

4. *Courageous shepherds know that selfishness is the enemy of spirituality and work hard to subdue their egos and ambitions.* They are unconcerned about their own personal visibility and do not pay much attention to who gets the credit. They recognize that the natural man with his ego and animal unconcern for others is the enemy of God, and they seek to become "as a child, submissive, meek, humble, patient, full of love, willing to submit to all things . . . even as a child doth submit to his father." (Mosiah 3:19.)

The Duke of Wellington was Britain's most celebrated military hero of the nineteenth century, honored in every possible way by a grateful king, people, and parliament. Despite all of the adulation showered on him, Wellington retained a healthy control over his ego. He never asked for promotion or honors. "Notwithstanding the numerous favours that I have received from the Crown, I have never solicited one. . . . I recommend to you the same conduct and patience," he wrote to a glory-seeker in 1813.

On his way to Portugal as a subordinate commander in 1806, Wellington placed firmly on record his understanding that obligation to duty transcends the pull of ego in those with true moral courage. A friend had urged Wellington to protest that he (Wellington) deserved a higher place in the army. Wellington demurred. "I have eaten of the King's salt," he said, "and therefore I conceive it to be my duty to serve with unhesitating zeal and cheerfulness, when and wherever the King or his government may think proper to employ me." (John Keegan, *The Mask of Command* [New York: Viking/Elisabeth Sifton Books, 1987], pp. 144, 163.)

Courageous shepherds who have mastered their egos will be repentant and humble, not puffed up with their own arrogance, recognizing the possibility that they may be wrong, or at least only partly right, aware of the fallibility built into the human race. They are leery about power, knowing that it intoxicates and finally enslaves its practitioner. They concur with Lord Acton's wise dictum "Power tends to corrupt and absolute power corrupts absolutely." (*Bartlett's Familiar Quotations,* p. 615.) They have the courage to treat power gingerly and not take themselves too seriously.

5. *Courageous shepherds develop both a willingness to change and the power to do so.* They use as their model the Holy One of Israel, the only perfect, sinless man, and strive with all of their hearts to "come unto Christ and be perfected in him." (Moroni 10:32.) Willingness to change comes only after recognition of the need to change and of the reality that all of us have much to be humble about. It thus is closely linked to repentance and humility.

Courageous shepherds know that change may be painful—and usually is. They recognize that to be fully effective, "mighty change" is needed. (Alma 5:14.) It must extend to a willingness to "give away all [our] sins to know" God. (See Alma 22:18.)

Courageous shepherds recognize that change may require forgiveness, complete and all encompassing. How difficult it can be to forgive someone who has harmed us! What courage it takes to overcome the tendency of the "natural man" to strike back, to exact revenge. Corrie Ten Boom, a devoted Christian, was active in the Dutch resistance against the Nazis during World War II. With sublime courage and at great personal danger, she and her beloved sister Betsie hid and helped numerous fugitives from Nazi terror. Eventually, the two sisters were betrayed and underwent the horror, deprivation, and brutality of a Nazi concentration camp. Through it all, both retained their total dedication to the Master, returning love for hatred, kindness for contempt. After the war ended and the long nightmare was behind her, Corrie underwent an experience that required her to forgive one who had done her and many others terrible wrong:

> It was at a church service in Munich that I saw him, the former S.S. man who had stood guard at the shower room door in the processing center at Ravensbruck. He was the first of our actual jailers that I had seen since that time. And suddenly it was all there—the roomful of mocking men, the heaps of clothing, Betsie's pain-blanched face.
>
> He came up to me as the church was emptying, beaming and bowing. "How grateful I am for your message, Fraulein," he said. "To think that, as you say, He has washed my sins away!"
>
> His hand was thrust out to shake mine. And I, who had preached so often to the people of Bloemendaal the need to forgive, kept my hand at my side.

Even as the angry, vengeful thoughts boiled through me, I saw the sin of them. Jesus Christ had died for this man; was I going to ask for more? Lord Jesus, I prayed, forgive me and help me to forgive him.

I tried to smile, I struggled to raise my hand. I could not. I felt nothing, not the slightest spark of warmth or charity. And so again I breathed a silent prayer. Jesus, I cannot forgive him. Give me Your forgiveness.

As I took his hand the most incredible thing happened. From my shoulder along my arm and through my hand a current seemed to pass from me to him, while into my heart sprang a love for this stranger that almost overwhelmed me.

And so I discovered that it is not on our forgiveness any more than on our goodness that the world's healing hinges, but on His. When He tells us to love our enemies, He gives, along with the command, the love itself." (*The Hiding Place* [New York: Bantam Books, 1974], p. 238.)

The shepherds of the Lord are quick to forgive the repentant sinner. In his efforts to establish the Church throughout all of the land of Nephi, Alma went to a city called Ammonihah. Amulek—"a man of no small reputation among all those who [knew him]," one who had also "acquired much riches," was commanded by an angel to take Alma into his house and feed him. (See Alma 10.) Amulek became converted to the gospel and began to serve as Alma's missionary companion. The two faithful servants of God soon found themselves contending against the lawyers and judges, who were "learned . . . and cunning," full of iniquity, and busily laying the foundations of the devil. Chief among those perverters of the ways of the righteous was one named Zeezrom, a man "expert in the devices of the devil." Alma and Amulek refuted Zeezrom's questions and preached the principles of the gospel. (See Alma 11.)

They spoke of Christ, who would come to redeem His people and take upon Himself the transgressions of those who believe on His name. They taught that the plan of redemption brings to pass the resurrection and that the repentant have a claim on mercy through Christ. Zeezrom began to tremble. (Alma 11:46.) The more he heard, the more he became convinced of the power of God. "And Zeezrom began to inquire of them diligently, that he might know more concerning the kingdom of God." (Alma 12:8.)

But the damage had been done. Zeezrom's lying words had been instrumental in hardening the hearts of the people. Alma and Amulek were thrown into prison, beaten, mocked, and starved. Their clothes were taken from them, and they were bound with strong cords. Many believers, including a repentant Zeezrom, whose "soul began to be harrowed up under a consciousness of his own guilt; yea, he began to be encircled about by the pains of hell" (Alma 14:6), fled from Ammonihah to the city of Sidom. Alma and Amulek, miraculously delivered from prison, also made their way to Sidom. There they found Zeezrom:

> Zeezrom lay sick at Sidom, with a burning fever, which was caused by the great tribulations of his mind on account of his wickedness, for he supposed that Alma and Amulek were no more; and he supposed that they had been slain because of his iniquity. And this great sin, and his many other sins, did harrow up his mind until it did become exceedingly sore, having no deliverance; therefore he began to be scorched with a burning heat.
>
> Now, when he heard that Alma and Amulek were in the land of Sidom, his heart began to take courage; and he sent a message immediately unto them, desiring them to come unto him.
>
> And it came to pass that they went immediately, obeying the message which he had sent unto them;

and they went in unto the house unto Zeezrom; and they found him upon his bed, sick, being very low with a burning fever; and his mind also was exceedingly sore because of his iniquities; and when he saw them he stretched forth his hand, and besought them that they would heal him.

And it came to pass that Alma said unto him, taking him by the hand: Believest thou in the power of Christ unto salvation?

And he answered and said: Yea, I believe all the words that thou hast taught.

And Alma said: If thou believest in the redemption of Christ thou canst be healed.

And he said: Yea, I believe according to thy words.

And then Alma cried unto the Lord, saying: O Lord our God, have mercy on this man, and heal him according to his faith which is in Christ.

And when Alma had said these words, Zeezrom leaped upon his feet, and began to walk; and this was done to the great astonishment of all the people; and the knowledge of this went forth throughout all the land of Sidom.

And Alma baptized Zeezrom unto the Lord; and he began from that time forth to preach unto the people. (Alma 15:3–12.)

Zeezrom had been forgiven. His sins were forgotten. The power of love had triumphed.

The Prophet Joseph also was quick to forgive those who had hurt him. One such was W. W. Phelps, whose betrayal had helped put Joseph into the Liberty Jail. To Phelps on July 22, 1840, Joseph wrote the following tender, loving letter—an epistle that tells much of the greatness of the Prophet's heart and his steadfast determination to follow the Christ, whose servant he was.

> I must say that it is with no ordinary feelings I endeavour to write a few lines to you. . . . You may in some measure realise what my feelings, as well

119

as Elder Rigdon's & Bro Hyrum's were when we read your letter, truly our hearts were melted into tenderness and compassion when we assertained your resolves & c

I can assure you I feel a disposition to act on your case in a manner that will meet the approbation of Jehovah (whose servant I am) and agreeably to the principles of truth and righteousness which have been revealed. . . .

It is true, that we have suffered much in consequence of your behavior — *the cup of gall already full enough* for mortals to drink, was indeed *filled to overflowing* when you turned against us: One with whom we had oft taken sweet council together, and enjoyed many refreshing seasons from the Lord "Had it been an enemy we could have borne it". . . . However the Cup has been drunk, the will of our heavenly Father has been done, and we are yet alive for which we thank the Lord. And having been delivered from the hands of wicked men by the mercy of our God, we say it is your privilidge to be delivered from the power of the Adversary — be brought into the liberty of God's dear children, and again take your stand among the Saints of the Most High, and by diligence humility and love unfeigned, commend yourself to our God and your God and to the church of Jesus Christ

Believing your confession to be real and your repentance genuine, I shall be happy once again to give you the right hand of fellowship, and rejoice over the returning prodigal.

Your letter was read to the Saints last Sunday and an expression of their feeling was taken, when it was unanimously resolved that W. W. Phelps should be received into fellowship.

"Come on dear Brother since the war is past,

For friends at first are friends again at last." (*The Personal Writings of Joseph Smith,* edited by Dean C. Jessee [Salt Lake City: Deseret Book Co., 1984], pp. 472–73; italics in original.)

While a young man serving as a member of the Council of the Twelve, Heber J. Grant learned an important lesson about forgiveness. A prominent man had been excommunicated from the Church. Years later he pled for rebaptism. President John Taylor referred the question to the apostles, indicating there would have to be unanimous agreement before the man could be baptized. Eventually, all but Elder Grant agreed. In conscience he could not do so; the man had acted so despicably. "My boy," said President Taylor, "stay with your convictions. . . . Don't you vote [for him] as long as you live, while you hold those ideas."

Later, feeling vindicated, Heber began to read from the scriptures. His book of Doctrine and Covenants opened to section 64. There he read: "Wherefore, I say unto you, that ye ought to forgive one another; for he that forgiveth not his brother his trespasses standeth condemned before the Lord; for there remaineth in him the greater sin. I, the Lord, will forgive whom I will forgive, but of you it is required to forgive all men." (D&C 64:9–10.)

Elder Grant returned to the office of President Taylor. "I have had a change of heart. . . . I have come to tell you [Brother So and So] can be baptized, so far as I am concerned."

President Taylor laughed. Said he, "Forgiveness is in advance of justice, where there is repentance; . . . to have in your heart the spirit of forgiveness and to eliminate from your hearts the spirit of hatred and bitterness, brings peace and joy." (*Conference Report,* October 1920, pp. 5–7.)

Why is it that God requires us to forgive "every man" (and every woman)? The answer is simple in concept, though difficult in execution: forgiveness is the key to peace in personal relationships. President Spencer W. Kimball spoke often of the healing power of forgiveness. He counseled that as we try to forgive what others have done to us, we begin to let go of all that has been hard to forgive in ourselves. The key to loving oneself—upon which our mental and spiritual health depends—lies in learning to forgive and love others.

The healing power of forgiveness is well illustrated by a story told by President Kimball:

> I was struggling with a community problem in a small ward . . . where two prominent men, leaders of the people, were deadlocked in a long and unrelenting feud. Some misunderstanding between them had driven them far apart with enmity. As the days, weeks, and months passed, the breach became wider. The families of each conflicting party began to take up the issue and finally nearly all the people of the ward were involved. Rumors spread and differences were aired and gossip became tongues of fire until the little community was divided by a deep gulf. I was sent to clear up the matter. After a long stake conference, lasting most of two days, I arrived at the frustrated community about six P.M., Sunday night, and immediately went into session with the principal combatants.
>
> How we struggled! How I pleaded and warned and begged and urged! Nothing seemed to be moving them. Each antagonist was so sure that he was right and justified that it was impossible to budge them.
>
> The hours were passing—it was now long after midnight, and despair seemed to enshroud the place; the atmosphere was still one of ill temper and ugliness. Stubborn resistance would not give way. Then it happened. I aimlessly opened my Doctrine and Covenants again and there before me it was. I had read it many times in past years and it had had no special meaning then. But tonight it was the very answer. It was an appeal and an imploring and a threat and seemed to be coming direct from the Lord. I read from the seventh verse on, but the quarreling participants yielded not an inch

until I came to the ninth verse. Then I saw them flinch, startled, wondering. Could that be right? The Lord was saying to us—to all of us—"Wherefore, I say unto you, that ye ought to forgive one another."

This was an obligation. They had heard it before. They had said it in repeating the Lord's Prayer. But now: " . . . for he that forgiveth not his brother his trespasses standeth condemned before the Lord . . . " (D&C 64:7–9)

In their hearts, they may have been saying: "Well, I might forgive if he repents and asks forgiveness, but he must make the first move." Then the full impact of the last line seemed to strike them: "For there remaineth in him the greater sin."

What? Does that mean I must forgive even if my antagonist remains cold and indifferent and mean? There is no mistaking it. . . .

Shocked, the two men sat up, listened, pondered a minute, then began to yield. This scripture added to all the others read brought them to their knees. Two A.M. and two bitter adversaries were shaking hands, smiling and forgiving and asking forgiveness. Two men were in a meaningful embrace. This hour was holy. Old grievances were forgiven and forgotten, and enemies became friends again. No reference was ever made again to the differences. The skeletons were buried, the closet of dry bones was locked and the key was thrown away, and peace was restored. (*The Teachings of Spencer W. Kimball* [Salt Lake City: Bookcraft, 1982], pp. 240–42.)

6. *The courageous shepherd knows that his own personal courage influences those around him.* Few leaders in history have had greater power to inspire others than had the Prophet Joseph Smith. It wasn't just his remarkable mind, his vigorous and dynamic physical constitution, his "native cheery temperament," or his great spirituality. There was something about Joseph that endeared people to him, that

bound his soul to theirs with hoops of steel. An episode in the very twilight of Joseph's life illustrates the great power of his example to inspire others to the point where they would lay down their lives for him if need be.

The terrible afternoon of the martyrdom, the jailer at Carthage jail, sensing no doubt that deviltry was afoot, suggested that Joseph and his companions enter the cell for their safety. Joseph turned to Willard Richards: "If we go into the cell, will you go in with us?" Willard's reply came without hesitation: "Brother Joseph you did not ask me to cross the river with you—you did not ask me to come to Carthage—you did not ask me to come to jail with you—and do you think I would forsake you now? But I will tell you what I will do; if you are condemned to be hung for treason, I will be hung in your stead, and you shall go free." Joseph indicated he could not allow Willard to sacrifice himself, but the doctor stoutly replied, "I will." (*History of the Church,* 6:616.)

Such is the power of example of a truly courageous leader!

Wise shepherds exemplify the courage they wish others to emulate. They try hard not to show fear or disquietude, though they may well feel them. They do not flag or fail; they struggle on to the end. They set a good example, knowing with Edmund Burke that "example is the school of mankind" (*Bartlett's Familiar Quotations,* p. 374) and a powerful teacher.

# CHAPTER FIVE

# The Persevering Shepherd

The year A.D. 1306 was one of the darkest in Scotland's long and often gloomy history. Edward I of England, aptly named "The Hammer of the Scots," invaded Scotland at the head of a powerful army. Soon the streets of Scotland's cities echoed to the clash and clatter of mailed soldiery. Noble and prominent families were imprisoned and tortured. Many were killed. The king of the Scots, Robert the Bruce, Lord of Kerrick, fled to his seigniory in the rough hills north of the English border. There he sought refuge in a cave, alone save for a solitary watcher in the heather charged with raising a warning should English troops appear.

Bruce was disconsolate, his spirit broken, his mood black and bitter. Many members of his family were imprisoned. Others had been hanged or drawn and quartered. The land and its people groaned under Edward's iron heel.

As he lay on his bed of heather in the gloomy recesses of the cave, Bruce's courage nearly failed him. What could he do, in the face of such terrible odds, to free his country from tyranny? Perhaps he should just give up, accept the inevitable, and fulfill his ambition to go as a humble pilgrim to the Holy Land.

Bruce's eyes fastened on a spider clinging precariously to a stone high in the mouth of the cave. He watched, first with idle curiosity and then with increasing interest, as the tiny beast attempted to swing on its gossamer strand to another perch several feet away. Six times the spider tried and failed. Finally, on the seventh attempt, it succeeded. Bruce vowed that if a lowly spider could persevere, the king of Scots could do no less. He fought on, with increasing power, finally ridding Scotland of her enemies at the Battle of Bannockburn in A.D. 1314. (See Ronald McNair Scott, *Robert the Bruce, King of Scots* [Edinburgh: Cannongate Publishing Ltd., 1982], p. 95.)

Like Bruce the Scottish king, faithful servants of truth and justice throughout the ages have understood that perseverance is a large part of their job. They have learned, by a combination of spirit-whisperings and experience, that dismal, even disastrous, failure can turn into scintillating success if only they can exert a little more effort and show a little more patience. They have learned never to give up, to let no temptation, frustration, discouragement, or disappointment deter them from the achievement of their goals. Victory has been the sweeter to them because and not in spite of the fact that they faced opposition and hardship. Life, they have found, is meant for struggle. (See Moses 3:22–25.)

Winston Churchill learned those lessons well. His magnificent wartime speeches, in which he "mobilized the English language and sent it into battle," echo again and again the theme of perseverance in the midst of "an ordeal of the most grievous kind." "We have before us," he said to the House of Commons on 13 May 1940, ". . . many, many long months of struggle and of suffering. . . . You ask what is our aim? I can answer in one word: Victory—victory at all costs, victory in spite of all terror, victory, however long and hard the road may be." (*Blood, Toil, Tears, and Sweat: The Speeches of Winston Churchill,* edited by David Cannadine [Boston: Houghton Mifflin Company, 1989], p. 149.)

In his Periclean tribute to the fighter pilots of the Royal Air Force (House of Commons, 20 August 1940), Churchill sounded this note of defiance and determination: "The road to victory may not be so long as we expect. But we have no right to count upon this. Be it long or short, rough or smooth, we mean to reach our journey's end." (Ibid., p. 182.) And in one of his most famous speeches, broadcast over the BBC on 9 February 1941, and addressed largely to American ears, the old lion growled again: "We shall not fail or falter; we shall not weaken or tire. Neither the sudden shock of battle, nor the long-drawn trials of vigilance and exertion will wear us down. Give us the tools, and we will finish the job." (Ibid., p. 213.)

Churchill understood that discouragement is a major foe of perseverance. Despondency, born of uncertainty and fear, saps courage and destroys resolution. It is so easy to lose a sense of proportion, to grow weary as we struggle through the "long, stern, scowling valley" (ibid., p. 214) of life, to lose heart as we contemplate what still remains undone. In the spring of 1941, when the tide of war continued to turn even more discouragingly against Britain, Churchill spoke again about the need not to lose heart nor weaken in resolution. "On, on to victory" was his recurring theme. He concluded his remarks, broadcast on the BBC on 27 April 1941, with these words from the poem "Say Not the Struggle Naught Availeth," by English poet Arthur Hugh Clough:

> For while the tired waves, vainly breaking,
>     Seem here no painful inch to gain,
> Far back, through creeks and inlets making,
>     Comes silent, flooding in, the main.
>
> And not by eastern windows only,
>     When daylight comes, comes in the light;

In front the sun climbs slow, how slowly,
But westward, look, the land is bright.
(Ibid., p. 224.)

Churchill knew, and through his prodigious rhetorical gifts inspired millions to come to understand, that perseverance is an important component of victory, in war and in life. Salvation will not be denied to those who with Olympian fortitude bear the pangs of misfortune and disappointment, in sure and certain confidence that in God's good time all will be made right.

The scriptures are replete with references to perseverance and endurance and contain many examples from the lives of great souls illustrating this powerful principle. The story of Job tells of the afflictions that befell a righteous man. One day Job had everything, it seemed, that a person could ever ask for—land, wealth, possessions, and, above all else, a loving family. Then the next day all was gone, and Job was left with nothing but tears and sorrow. "He hath stripped me of my glory, and taken the crown from my head. He hath destroyed me on every side," he lamented. (Job 19:9–10.) Job's faith in God, though sorely tried, remained strong: "Though he slay me, yet will I trust in him: . . . He also shall be my salvation: . . . For I know that my redeemer liveth, and that he shall stand at the latter day upon the earth: . . . yet in my flesh shall I see God." (Job 13:15–16; 19:25–26.)

Job's trials and tribulations exemplify the enigma of human suffering. He was a righteous man who had, so far as one can tell from the story, done nothing to warrant God's wrath. Why, then, was he made to suffer? Why indeed does any innocent person suffer? It is one of the puzzling paradoxes of human existence. I do not believe we know the answer in any degree of detail. Perhaps we are not meant to at this stage of our eternal existence but rather are to "live by faith." Experience, discipline and instruction are often cited as reasons why people are required to undergo suffering. One or more of these reasons may indeed partially explain some human suffering. But many have exquisite difficulty in understanding or even accepting why an innocent child, for example, should have to die slowly and in terrible pain as so many do daily. To many believers in God, unable to find in the teachings of their church answers to the paradox of suffering, religious faith reduces to stoical endurance and despair.

I do not even pretend to know in detail the full and complete answers to the enduring enigma of human suffering. But of several things I am sure. First, our Divine Parent, who loves us with a pure father's love, does not act toward us like a malicious child pulling the legs off a bug, just to watch it squirm in agony. He takes no pleasure from our suffering. Nor is He the author of all human suffering. "It is," said the Prophet Joseph, "an unhallowed principle to say that such and such have transgressed because they have been preyed upon by disease or death." (*Teachings of the Prophet Joseph Smith* [Salt Lake City: Deseret Book Co., 1976], p. 162.) We may not conclude that suffering results inevitably from the wrath of an angry God. God operates within a framework of eternal laws.

Secondly, Jesus, who suffered more than mortals can even contemplate, who bore the crushing burden of the sins of the world (D&C 19:18), knows of our suffering and has compassion for us (see 3 Nephi 17:6; D&C 64:2). He came to earth, not to end all suffering, but to end the *needless* suffering brought on by sin and to teach us that suffering need not be in vain. Through the infinite grace of His atonement, He will help us find the ability to endure, with wondrous promises of divine glory, of eternal joy with Him, if we do so. To a grievously afflicted prophet He proclaimed, "Thine adversity and thine afflictions shall be but a small moment; and then, if thou endure it well,

God shall exalt thee on high." (D&C 121:7–8.) And on an earlier occasion Jesus spoke these words of comfort and consolation, which have cheered and lifted so many over two millennia: "Come unto me, all ye that labour and are heavy laden, and I will give you rest. Take my yoke upon you, and learn of me; for I am meek and lowly in heart: and ye shall find rest unto your souls." (Matthew 11:28–29.)

Even though God is not the author of all human suffering, it is a measure of our devotion to His beloved son that from anguish and affliction can come spiritual enlightenment, soul growth, and a developing sense of self and of our relationship to God and Christ. The fire of affliction, which scars some souls, purifies and ennobles others, transforming them into celestial creatures filled with supernal joy. "All your losses will be made up to you in the resurrection, provided you continue faithful. By the vision of the Almighty I have seen it," said Joseph Smith, who knew more about struggle, pain, disappointment, and anguish than most. (*Teachings,* p. 296.)

There are, then, times when all we can do is hang on and endure to the end, recalling God's goodness to us in the past and His enduring love for us. In such circumstances Paul's words to the Corinthians take on added meaning: "Eye hath not seen, nor ear heard, neither have entered into the heart of man, the things which God hath prepared for them that love him." (1 Corinthians 2:9.) On such occasions we know, with Nephi, in whom we can trust. (See 2 Nephi 4:19, 34.)

But it is not my purpose to dwell at length on that aspect of perseverance that deals with the enduring of suffering. The shepherds of the flock, in common with all people, are inevitably required to undergo suffering and anguish. They must search the scriptures and the words of the living prophets to find their own personal answers to the perennial questions that surround suffering and be prepared to counsel members of their flock who cry in anguish, "Why me, or mine?" To provide that counsel requires both wisdom and compassion, neither of which come easily to the children of men. "How much better is it to get wisdom than gold! and to get understanding rather to be chosen than silver!" (Proverbs 16:16.)

## "Though Demons Oppose"

Perseverance has many faces, many aspects, all of which shepherds must learn. There is, of course, suffering, to which we have already alluded. But there is also the need to persevere in the face of opposition.

"Mormon-bashing" has long been a favorite pastime of some who for one reason or another disapprove of our doctrines and teachings. Since our earliest days, opposition, persecution, and misunderstanding have been our common companions. Perhaps we should not be too surprised. After all, since we truly are the Church of Jesus Christ, restored in its fullness at a pivotal point in world history, the dark, satanic forces that oppose *Him* can be expected to hurl themselves in fury also against *us*. And so they have, for more than a century and a half.

Nor can we expect that as we grow in size and become better known around the world, the opposition will become muted. Indeed, as the great winding-up scenes of human history progress, under an increasingly dark and somber sky, to their inevitable apocalyptic conclusion, Christ and His teachings will continue to be rejected by many, if not most. Sadly, even in many so-called Christian nations the preaching of the Word now struggles to be heard by societies whose members consider it not so much untrue or unbelievable as simply irrelevant. Of our time and place in history the Lord has declared: "They have strayed from mine ordinances, and have broken mine ever-

131

lasting covenant; they seek not the Lord to establish his righteousness, but every man walketh in his own way, and after the image of his own god, whose image is in the likeness of the world, and whose substance is that of an idol, which waxeth old and shall perish in Babylon, even Babylon the great, which shall fall." (D&C 1:15–16.)

In our time much of the opposition to the Church is verbal rather than physical. It was not always so and may not be again. Many of those who oppose us claim to be Christians, yet they use the most unchristian tactics in their attacks, unfettered by even reasonable concerns for fairness, accuracy, or balance in what they say and do. Some clearly feel threatened by our success, perhaps fearing that as we wax they will wane. In like manner the religious establishment during the decades following the death of Christ resented the message of Paul and its potential impact on their religious preeminence and economic well-being. Recall, for example, the instructive account of Paul's encounter with those who worshiped Diana, the goddess regarded as the source of the fruitful and nurturing powers of nature. Luke records:

> A certain man named Demetrius, a silversmith, which made silver shrines for Diana, brought no small gain unto the craftsmen; whom he called together with the workmen of like occupation, and said, Sirs, ye know that by this craft we have our wealth. Moreover ye see and hear, that not alone at Ephesus, but almost throughout all Asia, this Paul hath persuaded and turned away much people, saying that they be no gods, which are made with hands: So that not only this our craft is in danger to be set at nought; but also that the temple of the great goddess Diana should be despised, and her magnificence should be destroyed, whom all Asia and the world worshippeth. And when they heard these sayings, they were full of

wrath, and cried out, saying, Great is Diana of the
Ephesians. And the whole city was filled with confusion. (Acts 19:24–29.)

Is it any real wonder that Paul's detractors labeled him
"a pestilent fellow, and a mover of sedition among all the
Jews throughout the world, and a ringleader of the sect of
the Nazarenes"? (Acts 24:5.)

Perhaps those who call themselves Christian and harp
on what they claim are inconsistencies in our history and
doctrine need to be reminded that Christianity itself rests
upon very meager historic evidence. The miracles of Christ,
including His resurrection and atonement, the details of
His life and preachings, simply are not recorded in the
secular histories available to Christian and non-Christian
alike. Similarly, all Christians must wrestle with the fact
that the teachings and records found in the New Testament
(which, by the way, display their own internal minor inconsistencies) were written by friends and followers of
Jesus, not by objective historians. None of this should
be of inordinate concern to any of us, Mormon or non-
Mormon. The validity of the Christian message rests on
spiritual, rather than secular, foundations.

Yet we must not dwell too long on those who are our
professional detractors, who make a living (often a very
good living!) by criticizing the Mormons. They will always
be with us and will be dealt with in the Lord's good time
and in His way. They will not have any appreciable impact
on the work, "for the eternal purposes of the Lord shall
roll on, until all his promises shall be fulfilled." (Mormon
8:22.) Elder Marvin J. Ashton has wisely reminded us that
"no religion, group, or individual can prosper over an
extended period of time with fault-finding as their foundation." (*Ensign,* November 1982, p. 63.)

We must be ever mindful of the need to be "swift to
hear, slow to speak, slow to wrath: for the wrath of man

worketh not the righteousness of God." (James 1:19–20.) We must avoid like the plague the common tendency to strike back in anger at those who unjustly attack us. We must never revile the revilers (see D&C 19:30) but rather "declare glad tidings" in "all humility," preaching "repentance and faith on the Savior, and remission of sins by baptism, and by fire, yea, even the Holy Ghost." (D&C 19:29–31.)

There are many—the good, honest, fair-minded people of the world—who sincerely want to hear more about us, "for there are many yet on the earth among all sects, parties, and denominations, who are blinded by the subtle craftiness of men, whereby they lie in wait to deceive, and who are only kept from the truth because they know not where to find it." (D&C 123:12.)

In dealing effectively with opposition, there are several great messages the Lord's shepherds must struggle to have presented. Fair-minded people everywhere will respect them, though not all will accept them. They include the following:

1. *We are Christians.* In an age when Christ is denigrated, as the scriptures foretold He would be, our message is that He lives! As did the Nephites of old, "we talk of Christ, we rejoice in Christ, we preach of Christ, we prophesy of Christ, and we write according to our prophecies, that our children may know to what source they may look for a remission of their sins." (2 Nephi 25:26.)

The scriptures, particularly the blessed Book of Mormon, are filled with that celestial central message. It is found on every page of the Book of Mormon. Indeed, the name of Christ, in one form or another, appears on average every 1.7 verses in the Nephite scriptures!

2. *We care for others.* At the end of the day, our belief in Christ will best be reflected to others by the extent to which we practice what we preach. Elder Neal A. Maxwell

has reminded us: "Overall, the perception of us as a Church and people will improve in direct proportion to the degree to which we mirror the Master in our lives. No media effort can do as much good—over the sweep of time—as can *believing, behaving,* and *serving* members of the Church! The eloquence of such examples will be felt and seen in any culture or community." (Address to Area Office Public Communications Directors, April 9, 1985.)

As always, Jesus said it best: "He that hath my commandment, and keepeth them, he it is that loveth me." (John 14:21.) Church members and units demonstrate concern for others by reaching out through Christian service and involvement in the community. Christlike service breaks down barriers and melts prejudice and misunderstanding. The following story, taken from the *Ensign* a few years ago, illustrates the point:

When Robert Henry Daines and his wife, Anna, moved into their first home in a strange town, they were warned that the town was very anti-Mormon. The Dainses soon noticed that their children were not invited to play in neighbor's houses. When they tried to rent a room for Church meetings at the local YMCA, the board of directors responded by saying that the facilities could not be used by Mormons.

Instead of moving away from such prejudice, Robert and Anna decided to serve the community and perhaps to win acceptance. They enrolled their oldest son in the YMCA, and Sister Daines joined the YMCA Mother's Auxiliary. She raised funds, cleaned up after parties, and chaperoned dances. Since she worked the hardest, she was soon asked to be the president of the Mother's Auxiliary. After working hard for two years, she was asked to run for the YMCA board of directors. She won without opposition, joining the very council that only a few years before had refused to let the Mormons rent a room in the building. While on the board of directors, she worked to change the tradition of an all-night drinking party following high school graduation to a chaperoned party and dance at the YMCA. This new tradition continued for many years. After serving three years on the board, she was reelected. One of her fellow board members confessed, "I must tell you . . . that I was the one who spearheaded the campaign not to let the Mormons use this hall. I didn't know anything good about the Mormons. . . . I feel that I owe you an apology after seeing what fine people you are."

Meanwhile, Robert and Anna Daines had also joined the Parent Teacher Association. They worked hard and soon became co-presidents of the PTA at their local elementary school. After heading a committee that completed an impressive two-year study for the PTA, Brother Daines was urged to run for the Board of Education. There was quite a bit of talk against the idea of a Mormon running the schools; however, he won the election. As president of the school board, Robert Daines worked with the local minister to reverse the policy of holding high school graduation in the local Protestant church. Some students, not belonging to this church, were forbidden by their churches to attend their own graduation. Brother Daines arranged with the church leaders to hold graduation in the school gymnasium. He also arranged for the monsignor of the Catholic church, the minister of the black congregation, the Jewish rabbi, and various Protestant ministers to participate on the program. Respect and acceptance for Brother Daines and the Mormons increased among the leaders of these churches. Brother Daines was reelected twice—the last time by the largest majority in the school board's history.

Eventually, every one of the Daines children married in the temple. All their sons and sons-in-law served missions. They have served in quorum presidencies, bishoprics, and stake presidencies. When, at long last, a stake was organized in their community, Robert Daines was called as counselor and later as stake president. Other stakes were created, and he again served as stake president.

Instead of sheltering their children or running from prejudice, Robert and Anna Daines had won acceptance and had exerted significant leadership and influence in their community. (See Orson Scott Card, "Neighborliness: Daines Style," *Ensign*, April 1977, pp. 19–22.)

3. *There are plain and precious differences in the restored gospel.* We are *not* just another Christian denomination. We proclaim (hopefully with "boldness but not overbearance," Alma 38:12) that the gospel of Christ has been restored *in its fullness* to the earth and that this restoration was necessary precisely because plain and precious truths and the necessary priesthood authority had been lost. (See 1 Nephi 13:26–29, 34–40.) That is our message. We should not shrink from telling it because we want others to like us. We have no wish to offend—and we must be sensitive to the feelings of others—but we cannot subscribe to the homogenized ecumenicism which proclaims that all denominations and beliefs are equally favored of God. All roads may indeed lead to Rome, but they most emphatically don't all lead to the celestial kingdom! Elder Dallin H. Oaks has reminded us: "The value to the world of the Restored Gospel of Jesus Christ lies in its savour, its difference from the rest of Christianity and from the rest of the world. If we fail to communicate that difference, that unique addition we can make to the understanding and authority of the rest of Christianity, we will have lost our value to the world and to the kingdom and will be 'good for nothing, but to be cast out, and to be trodden under foot of men'

(Matthew 5:13)." (Address to Regional Representatives, April 5, 1985.)

4. *Church programs sustain and build families and individuals.* President David O. McKay used to say that the purpose of the Church is to "make bad men good and good men better." We must speak out boldly about the importance of righteous, loving families — the heart of a free, just, and peaceful society. We must let others know that Church programs help to sustain and build families and individuals. Family home evenings, personal and family prayer, scripture study, family history programs, our emphasis on self-reliance, all of our church facilities and activities have as their purpose the development and maintenance of strong, happy, and righteous families and individuals. This emphasis on the family will, of course, be ridiculed and laughed at by some; but most people, even many of those who are not conventionally religious, place a high value on family life.

The other side of the coin is equally important. We *must* speak out in plainness to oppose those trends and tendencies in our society that erode and degrade the moral fabric of individuals, families, and communities. Perhaps no one in the history of the Church has felt more deeply or spoken more plainly about the importance of the family than has President Ezra Taft Benson. By example and in numerous presentations over many years he has provided us with clear directions. "Come, listen to a prophet's voice, and hear the word of God," we sing. (*Hymns,* no. 21.) With that message ringing in our ears, let us proclaim the Prophet's words on the importance of family to the world — boldly, nobly, and independently.

Finally, if shepherds are to help bring the Church forth out of obscurity, at times they will have to act rapidly and decisively to set the record straight — to correct blatant, even malicious misunderstandings. A recent example of the effectiveness of such action comes from England. Not too long ago, a sixty-four-year-old widow in the town of Bedford was attacked in her apartment by two men who robbed her. The police described the two men as smartly dressed in dark blue suits and as being in their early thirties. One had a moustache and poorly cut, ragged hair. They spoke in local rather than American accents. Although nothing in this description supports the notion that the attackers were Mormon missionaries, the local newspaper headlined its story, "Mormon Theory on Raid Ordeal" and reported that "detectives believe the two assailants could be Mormons, some of whom are thought to be currently in town."

The Church's public communications director in the area, Bryan Grant, took prompt and effective action to counter this libelous calumny. A check with the local police quickly brought out the fact that *they* did not implicate Mormon missionaries in the crime. The newspaper editor was approached and politely but firmly reminded of the need to be fair in what he printed. A retraction headlined "Mormons Not Guilty" quickly ensued. Of perhaps greater importance, Brother Grant sent a letter to the newspaper editor involved, thanking him for acting promptly in putting out a corrected story and indicating our appreciation for the responsible way he acted. Furthermore, Brother Grant pointed out to the editor that the Bedford Branch of the Church dates back to 1837 and is in fact the second branch founded in the British Isles. He sent the editor a thousand-word story on the history of the Bedford Branch and included a couple of photos.

This story illustrates several important truths about dealing with opposition. First, we have every right to defend ourselves against patently untrue, malicious attacks on our integrity. After all, if such attacks were directed against other religious groups—Jews or Catholics or many

139

others for that matter—there would be a public outcry and the perpetrators would be brought to public scorn. Fair-minded people everywhere will recognize that we, too, have the right to respond calmly and fairly to those who revile us. Second, if we are to respond, we must do so promptly. Given the normal life of most newspaper stories, failure to respond quickly is a virtual guarantee that our view will not be heard. Finally, if we respond, we must be effective in what we do—going beyond simple denial to provide positive declarations and useful information in a friendly, helpful, noncensorial way. Victories are not won by denials only.

The challenges from opposition to the work of Christ will increase over the coming years. So, too, will the opportunities to serve and help in moving the kingdom forward. In all that we do, we must convey a quiet determination to do the Lord's work, putting into action President Spencer W. Kimball's famous dictum *"Do it!"* We must portray the quiet dignity that befits those who are servants of the Master.

## The Struggle to Persevere with Ourselves

The letters of the Apostle Paul to the branches of the Church he was instrumental in founding throughout Asia Minor constitute the major part of the incomplete record we have of the early Church in those tumultuous three decades after the death and resurrection of Jesus. Fragmentary though they are, Paul's writings provide vivid insight into the struggles of the leaders to keep the infant Church true to the doctrines established by the Savior. Even in Paul's time the dark stain of apostasy had begun to seep into the Church as it tried to accommodate a wicked and perverse world. One of the saddest statements in all of Paul's writings is found in his second letter to his beloved

Timothy: "Demas hath forsaken me," wrote Paul from Rome, "having loved this present world." (2 Timothy 4:10.)

I have often wondered and worried about what happened to Demas. He is mentioned in two of Paul's earlier letters—to the Colossians and to Philemon. He had obviously been a strong and beloved companion in the work; but lacking perseverance, he did not endure to the end. Why did he pack up and leave? Were his feelings hurt in some way? Did he perhaps tire of the discipline needed for Christian commitment? Perhaps he was seduced by one or more of the temptations of the flesh. Perhaps a bottle or a woman led him away. Or perhaps it was one or more of the deadly quartet composed of pride, property, power, and prominence. We just don't know. Whether from a sense of propriety or from loyalty to Demas, Paul's record is silent beyond that one terse, tragic comment: "Demas hath forsaken me."

For whatever reason, Demas did not persevere. Losing his grip on the iron rod, he fell away into the dark and filthy torrent of the world. How Paul must have wept and grieved over Demas, undoubtedly remembering the Savior's admonition to seek after and bring back the lost lamb. He must have wanted to reach out to Demas in love, anxious to forgive, pleading and praying and inviting him to come back.

Though our world of the twentieth century is much different from that in which Paul lived, there are many who represent the modern counterparts of Demas. Having loved too much this present world, they slip away from the Church and kingdom of God, forsaking the sweet and satisfying fruits of fellowship with the Saints for the tinsel and glitter of the world's tawdry counterfeits. Some have been hurt or feel neglected. Some feel guilty, unable to forgive themselves for previous transgressions even though their Father in heaven remembers their sin no

141

more. To all who transgress, the devil whispers the deadly lie that their sins are such they can never be forgiven, and thus he leads them away into darkness.

Unless human nature has changed a lot more than I think it has in the past two thousand years, I venture to guess that the cause of Demas' failure to endure to the end probably related in some way to a lack of self-mastery, an unwillingness to "give away all [his] sins to know [God]." (Alma 22:18.) The struggle to control one's self, to master the natural man, is a struggle many unfortunately lose with dire results. "He that hath no rule over his own spirit is like a city that is broken down, and without walls." (Proverbs 25:28.) Each must contend daily with the temptations of the flesh in all their alluring enticement. The struggle ends only with the grave, though it may take different forms during the various phases of life.

Even the prophets of God struggle to master themselves. Indeed, it may safely be said they would not be called and sustained in their holy calling in the absence of that mastery.

The great Nephi wept at his human weakness: "O wretched man that I am! Yea, my heart sorroweth because of my flesh; my soul grieveth because of mine iniquities. I am encompassed about, because of the temptations . . . which do so easily beset me. And when I desire to rejoice, my heart groaneth because of my sins." (2 Nephi 4:17–19.)

Nephi's sentiments are similar to those of Paul, who also wrote with deep emotion and obvious personal experience of the inner struggle between the flesh and the spirit. Wrote Paul: "I know that in me (that is, in my flesh) dwelleth no good thing: for to will is present with me; but how to perform that which is good I find not. For the good that I would I do not: but the evil which I would not, that I do. . . . For I delight in the law of God after the inward man: But I see another law in my members, warring against the law of my mind, and bringing me into captivity to the law of sin which is in my members. O wretched man that I am! who shall deliver me from the body of this death?" (Romans 7:18–19, 22–24.)

The cultivation of Christlike qualities is a lifelong struggle, demanding and relentless in calling forth the very best in us, stretching our souls. "Who has a harder battle than he who strives to conquer himself? And this must be our endeavour, in a word, to subdue ourselves, day by day to gain the mastery of self and make progress towards something better." (Thomas à Kempis, *The Imitation of Christ*, translated by E. M. Blaiklock [London: Hodder and Stoughton, 1979], p. 26.) The struggle for self-mastery is not a battle we fight only once. In one form or another, we must strive every day of our lives if we are to toil the pilgrim's path to perfection. Thorns, briars, and noxious weeds abound along the path. Yet He who stands with beckoning arms at the end of our journey gives us daily strength as we look to Him for guidance.

It is in the scriptures and the words of the living prophets that we find the lessons required to teach us mastery of self, the template upon which we can build a celestial life. Mastery of self is a major recurring theme of Christ and His prophets. Recall these glorious words of Alma to his son Helaman:

> O remember, remember, my son Helaman, how strict are the commandments of God. And he said: If ye will keep my commandments ye shall prosper in the land — but if ye keep not his commandments ye shall be cut off from his presence. . . . I tell you by the spirit of prophecy, that if ye transgress the commandments of God . . . ye shall be delivered up unto Satan, that he may sift you as chaff before the wind. But if ye keep the commandments of God, and do with these things which are sacred according to that which the Lord doth command

143

you, behold, no power of earth or hell can take them from you, for God is powerful to the fulfilling of all his words. (Alma 37:13, 15–16.)

To another son, Corianton, who had fallen into the coils of sin, Alma gave this fatherly counsel:

> Repent and forsake your sins, and go no more after the lusts of your eyes, but cross yourself in all these things; for except ye do this ye can in nowise inherit the kingdom of God. . . . I command you to take it upon you to counsel with your elder brothers in your undertakings; for behold, thou art in thy youth, and ye stand in need to be nourished by your brothers. And give heed to their counsel. . . . Suffer not yourself to be led away by any vain or foolish thing; suffer not the devil to lead away your heart again. . . . Refrain from your iniquities; . . . turn to the Lord with all your mind, might, and strength; . . . acknowledge your faults. . . . Seek not after riches nor the vain things of this world; for behold, you cannot carry them with you. (Alma 39:9–14.)

President Kimball spoke often of the benefits of self-mastery that come from reading the scriptures. Said he: "I find that when I get casual in my relationships with divinity and when it seems that no divine ear is listening and no divine voice is speaking, that I am far, far away. If I immerse myself in the scriptures the distance narrows and the spirituality returns. I find myself loving more intensely those whom I must love with all my heart and mind and strength, and loving them more, I find it easier to abide their counsel." (*The Teachings of Spencer W. Kimball* [Salt Lake City: Bookcraft, 1982], p. 135.)

President Kimball knew, as have all the prophets, that in the struggle to master one's self, service to others is the key. It drives away the selfishness that is the enemy of spirituality, the opponent of righteousness. To the extent we serve others, our souls grow, and we attain mastery of ourselves, eschewing self-indulgence and fleeting pleasure for the stern, sweet joy of obedience to divine commandments.

The lives of many of the pioneer Saints provide vivid examples of the sanctifying power of service. Consider Aurelia Spencer Rogers, whose life was as humble and unpretentious as that of the legendary country mouse. She knew much of sacrifice and sorrow. In the winter of 1845–46, the Rogers family, along with the other Saints in Nauvoo, were forced to flee the city. Aurelia was then a girl of only eleven years. She wrote of that horrendous experience: "My mother had scarcely recovered from a spell of sickness, which followed the death of little Chloe (a baby sister), and was illy prepared to stand the cold weather and rough roads we had to travel over in the fore part of the journey. She therefore gradually sank from the effects of a severe cold and soon died. As we had only traveled a distance of thirty miles, her body was taken back to Nauvoo and buried. . . . This was my first great sorrow. We missed her very much." (*Life Sketches* [Salt Lake City: George Q. Cannon & Sons, 1898], pp. 34–35, 41.)

While the family was at Winter Quarters, Orson Spencer, Aurelia's father, was sent to fulfill a mission in England as editor of the *Millennial Star*. The children were left largely to look after themselves. Aurelia's fourteen-year-old sister Ellen became "the little mother." It was hard going. In reflecting on that difficult period in her life, Aurelia wrote:

> The winter having been uncommon in its severity, our horse and all our cows but one had died, therefore we had no milk nor butter; our provisions had also nearly given out, so that in the spring and summer following, we really suffered for something to eat; part of the time having nothing but corn-meal, which was stirred up with water and

145

baked on a griddle. Many a night I have gone to bed without supper having to wait until I was hungry enough to eat our poor fare. . . . There was no need of our family suffering for food, if the money father sent us had been received; but although the money failed to reach us, the letters received from our dear parent were a great comfort to us. (Ibid., pp. 50–51.)

The Spencer children traveled in President Brigham Young's company to the Salt Lake Valley in the summer of 1848. Aurelia's trials were far from finished when she arrived in the Valley. In recalling her life, she wrote:

In the summer of 1855, grasshoppers came in swarms, destroying the crops and gardens. . . . This caused much suffering. Flour was scarce, and many of the people lived on bran bread. My husband sold a horse for $20, with which he bought a little flour; but for a short time we fared no better than those who lived on the bran diet. (Ibid., p. 155.)

My fourth child, Howard was born July 27th, 1859. He was a bright healthy baby, but was taken sick and died, when fourteen months old. I had been so happy previous to this; the trials of poverty and sickness that we had passed through were nothing compared to this great sorrow that had overtaken me; and I mourned for my babe. . . . I was ill most of the next winter, and came near to death a number of times; yet notwithstanding I longed to see my babe, I did not wish to die, but wanted to live to rear my other children, realizing what it was to be left motherless at an early age. I prayed to the Lord constantly, and told Him if He would spare my life, I would try to keep His commandments and serve Him to the best of my ability. My prayers were answered, and I lived to have eight more children, but only raised four out of the eight; therefore my life has been intermingled with joys and sorrows. (Pp. 163–64.)

My tenth child, which we named William, was born on the 31st of May, 1871, and only lived until the 17th of August, then died of cholera infantum. . . . this making three children that I had lost in succession. Of my ten children only five remained. It seemed indeed as if my last hope was gone, as I felt that I had no health or strength to have any more family. And I almost lost faith in God. . . . Subsequently, when pondering these things over, I felt that perhaps all the people of God would have to pass through certain ordeals to prove whether they would trust in Him to the end. (Pp. 179–80.)

During all the long years of her life as wife and mother in Farmington, Utah, Aurelia did the washing by hand, baked as many as twelve loaves of bread a day, sewed all the clothes for her large family, worked in the fields, and supported her family while her husband Thomas (a Scot from Falkirk who had emigrated to Canada and thence to Nauvoo and the West) was on a mission.

Aurelia's name is famous in the history of the Church because of her great service to children. She had noted the need for an organization for little boys wherein "they could be taught everything good, and how to behave." (P. 207.) Approval was received from President John Taylor to set up an organization for children, to include both boys and girls. The organization was called "Primary," and on August 11, 1878, Sister Rogers was set apart by Bishop John W. Hess as president of the very first Primary of the Church. For the rest of her life, she devoted herself to service in the Primary organization. Only the angels can tell the results of her selfless service. One thing, however, is certain: millions of children and their parents have been blessed by Primary, the organization whose purpose, to help parents teach their children the gospel of Christ and help them to learn to live it, is encapsulated in this single, glorious verse: "All thy children shall be taught of the Lord; and great shall be the peace of thy children." (3 Nephi 22:13.)

## Applying the Principles: Guidelines for Shepherds

1. *"By patient continuance in well doing . . . "* It is so easy for the Lord's shepherds to become impatient, to expect instant results, immediate success. Then, when that doesn't happen, one may be tempted to say, "I'll do it myself," or "Release that person and find somebody who can get the job done." When leaders push and prod, when they lose patience with others, they cease to lead; and even if the work gets done, it may well not be "in the Lord's way."

Impatience is one of the serious spiritual maladies of our age. Modern society encourages haste and the impatience that so often accompanies it. If you don't believe me, just observe the impatience etched on the faces of a crowd of people pushing and shoving their way onto a bus or subway train. Too often we rush here and there, always in a hurry, not really listening to others or to the Spirit, not taking the time to savor life, to enjoy its goodness, or to exercise the patience to wait. The lives of too many increasingly resemble a kind of speeded-up version of the popular television cartoon character, the Road Runner.

Without patience there can be no perseverance, no enduring in faith. As Paul wrote to the Romans, eternal life comes to those who "by patient continuance in well doing seek for glory and honour." (Romans 2:7.) We must learn to wait, to give people time to catch the vision, to not lose faith in them if they don't at first fully succeed, to never give up. There is, of course, a time to act; but there is also a time to be patient, to follow the divinely appointed rhythm of life. These beloved words from Ecclesiastes perhaps say it best: "To every thing there is a season, and a time to every purpose under the heaven: a time to be born, and a time to die; a time to plant, and a time to pluck up that which is planted." (Ecclesiastes 3:1–2.)

As they contemplate the vast amount of work that has to be done to prepare a Zion people for the second coming of the Master, as they view with sorrow the tendency among many to disregard sacred things, leaders may betimes get discouraged. On that subject, President Joseph F. Smith had these wise words of counsel:

> What shall we do? Shall we quit because there are those with whom we come in contact who are not willing to rise to the standard to which we seek to exalt them? No! Someone has said that the Lord hates a quitter, and there should be no such thing as quitting when we put our hands to the plow to save men, to save souls, to exalt mankind, to inculcate principles of righteousness and establish them in the hearts of those with whom we are associated, both by precept and by example. There must be no such thing as being discouraged. Under certain conditions and circumstances, we may fail to accomplish the object we have in view with reference to this individual or the other individual, or a number of individuals that we are seeking to benefit, to uplift, to purify, to get into their hearts the principles of justice, of righteousness, of virtue and of honor, that would fit them to inherit the kingdom of God; to associate with angels. . . . If you fail, never mind. Go right on; try it again; try it somewhere else. Never say quit. Do not say it cannot be done. . . . The word "fail" ought to be expunged from our language and our thoughts. We do not fail when we seek to benefit the erring, and they will not listen to us. (*Gospel Doctrine* [Salt Lake City: Deseret Book Co., 1986], pp. 132–33.)

On another occasion, President Smith had this to say

about patience in leadership: "In leaders undue impatience and a gloomy mind are almost unpardonable, and *it sometimes takes almost as much courage to wait as to act*. It is to be hoped, then, that the leaders of God's people, and the people themselves, will not feel that they must have at once a solution of every question that arises to disturb the even tenor of their ways."(*Gospel Doctrine*, p. 156; italics added.)

Patience, then, is one of the attributes of great leaders who know when to drive forward with all their strength and when to practice patient forbearance, recognizing that many of life's problems yield only to time. There are few quick solutions to major problems.

Whenever we get impatient with others or with ourselves, frustrated with the slow progress of our own drive toward the goal of individual perfection or that of those for whom we bear a shepherd's responsibility, perhaps it would be well to remember that there is a divinely determined velocity to the Lord's work. God has His own timetable that does not always agree with our desires. The very fact that we are required to wait, to endure with patience, to acquire wisdom and understanding "line upon line, precept upon precept" (D&C 98:12) is part of the Lord's developmental plan for us. He knows that it takes time for us to understand and apply in our lives the lofty celestial principles of the glorious gospel. Stalwart souls do not grow like tomatoes forced in a greenhouse, but slowly and gradually: "Behold, thus saith the Lord God: I will give unto the children of men line upon line, precept upon precept, here a little and there a little; and blessed are those who hearken unto my precepts, and lend an ear unto my counsel, for they shall learn wisdom; for unto him that receiveth I will give more; and from them that shall say, We have enough, from them shall be taken away even that which they have." (2 Nephi 28:30.)

It is not that God does not desire to give us more of His eternal truths. He longs to enlighten our minds with the celestial visions of the eternities. The Prophet Joseph Smith, God's mighty messenger of the restoration, longed to impart to others divine knowledge entrusted to him. Said he, "It is my meditation all the day and more than my meat and drink to know how I shall make the Saints of God to comprehend the visions that roll like an overflowing surge, before my mind." (*The Words of Joseph Smith,* p. 196.)

"I could explain a hundred fold more than I ever have of the glories of the kingdoms manifested to me in the vision, were I permitted, and were the people prepared to receive them. The Lord deals with this people as a tender parent with a child, communicating light and intelligence and the knowledge of his ways as they can bear it." (*History of the Church,* 5:402.)

Faithful shepherds, be patient: God's truth *will* prevail, both in the world and in the hearts of humble souls who "come unto Christ, and [are] perfected in him." (Moroni 10:32.)

2. *Look beyond the superficial to see the divine potential in people.* Wise shepherds, as they persevere with members of their flock, will learn to look beyond first impressions to the gold that lies at the base of every human soul.

My thoughts turn to a young man, a very much less active member of the Church when found by faithful home teachers. Brother Bob Smith, as we shall call him, had been baptized at age eight, primarily because of the efforts of his faithful grandmother, one of the pioneer members in her Church branch. But from that point on, Bob had essentially no contact with the Church. His parents were totally inactive, and their life-style was hardly celestial, to say the least. Like too many others, Bob drifted away from the Church. His nonmember friends were no better than they needed to be. He joined a motorcycle gang and spent raucous evenings and weekends in their company. Eventually Bob married but still retained his ties to his motorcycle buddies, wearing a grease-stained leather jacket over the shoulders of which his long unkempt hair cascaded.

Periodically Bob's name was discussed at ward council meetings. Whenever that happened, a subdued sigh went around the table: no sense in contacting that family; everyone knew *their* history.

But a young home teacher, who took seriously his errand from the Lord, decided to call on Bob Smith. When he arrived, he found Bob out in the yard repairing a motorcycle. Perhaps surprisingly, Bob was cordial, in his rough way, and listened attentively to the home teaching message. A couple of weeks later he accepted an invitation to come to priesthood meeting, creating somewhat of a stir when he arrived unshaven, in his leather motorcycle jacket. The priesthood leaders in the ward saw beyond Bob's appearance, recognizing in him a young man who desperately wanted to make something of himself and had a deep spiritual hunger. Soon Bob's appearance changed. He cut his hair and came to church neatly dressed, with his young wife and two small children.

Bob's faith grew by leaps and bounds. Soon he was called as a home teacher, then as a Sunday School teacher. It wasn't long before Bob and his family were sealed in the temple. He remains true and faithful, honoring his priesthood and striving to live the commandments. I'm convinced that Bob would not be where he is today without the perseverance of dedicated priesthood leaders who looked not on his countenance but "on the heart."

The renowned Christian philosopher C. S. Lewis possessed rare insight into our divine potential, as evidenced by this passage from his book *Mere Christianity:*

> The command *Be ye perfect* is not idealistic gas.

Nor is it a command to do the impossible. He is going to make us into creatures that can obey that command. He said (in the Bible) that we were "gods" and He is going to make good His words. If we let Him—for we can prevent Him, if we choose—He will make the feeblest and filthiest of us into a god or goddess, a dazzling, radiant, immortal creature, pulsating all through with such energy and joy and wisdom and love as we cannot now imagine, a bright stainless mirror which reflects back to God perfectly (though, of course, on a smaller scale) His own boundless power and delight and goodness. The process will be long and in parts very painful; but that is what we are in for. Nothing less. He meant what He said. ([Glasgow: Fount/William Collins Sons and Co., 1977], p. 172.)

As they persevere with people, never giving up on them, wise shepherds will, of course, recognize that all do not start with the same talents, nor do they all progress at the same speed. Yet all are God's children, equally beloved by Him. Each has his or her own strengths and weaknesses. Each faces unique challenges and opportunities. If the Lord's shepherds are to truly be patient with the flock, they must know each sheep intimately. In portraying Himself as the Good Shepherd, Jesus taught with superb skill the important lesson that the shepherd must know each member of the flock. The shepherd, said Jesus, "calleth his own sheep by name, and leadeth them out. And when he putteth forth his own sheep, he goeth before them, and the sheep follow him: for they know his voice. And a stranger will they not follow, but will flee from him: for they know not the voice of strangers." (John 10:3–5.) As with all else, the Good Shepherd provides the pattern for faithful undershepherds to follow.

3. *Shepherds must safeguard and replenish their strength, or they will "surely wear away."* Wise Jethro recognized Moses'

153

propensity to do too much, to become involved with every detail, to answer every question.

Unless they are very careful, modern-day shepherds can readily fall into the same trap as did Moses, believing that they are indispensable, wearing themselves out trying to be all things to all people. At best, this is foolish and futile; at worst, an ego trip that fosters pride and spiritual arrogance on the part of the shepherd and dangerous dependency on the part of the flock. If they are to endure, shepherds must learn how and what to delegate. They must not attempt to settle every question, to be the inexhaustible fount of all knowledge. They must learn to set priorities and manage their time effectively. Failing that, they will surely wear away, and those they strive to lead will ultimately suffer too.

Time available to shepherds is limited. There is absolutely no stretch to it. It is unchangeable; once expended it is gone forever. For the purposes of this discussion, let us consider three different types of time: leader-imposed time, system-imposed time, and self-imposed time, which may be divided into subordinate-imposed and discretionary time.

*Leader-imposed time.* Expenditure of this type of time by a shepherd results from requests by his or her ecclesiastical leader. The shepherd dares not ignore them. He who calls the shepherd has the authority (and indeed the responsibility!) to ask him or her to do certain things.

*System-imposed time.* This type of time expenditure is imposed by the demands of the organization for essential financial systems, membership attendance reporting systems, meetings, and so on. Shepherds cannot ignore needs to deal with system-imposed time. Neither the Church nor the Lord will let them do so. They must learn the "system" and make it work for them. Is it asking too much, for example, to suggest that a Relief Society president learn the manual? Reports must be used as management tools to help shepherds do their work.

*Self-imposed time.* With subordinate-imposed time, the shepherd must determine whether he or she will accept these demands. In response to one who says *"We've* got a problem" when really he or she has the problem, the shepherd could appropriately think, "Whose responsibility is this problem, really?" Shepherds should aim to give away as many problems as possible and to keep only those that can't be given to anybody else, because the shepherd bears a unique responsibility to provide help. A glaring example of a compulsive problem grabber is the bishop who does all of his counselors' thinking and acting. Either he does all their work, or he says "I'll take up your problem with Brother Jones, my counselor responsible for Primary." Both responses are wrong. Shepherds should gently but firmly encourage their counselors, teachers, and others to accept responsibility. Shepherds must not think for them. They must encourage them not to bring problems but rather solutions. Shepherds must help all they can but not "pull the trigger" for others.

Wise shepherds can also make routine the repetitive aspects of the work: agendas, meeting times, minutes of meetings (including follow-up), and so on.

Shepherds should use self-imposed discretionary time for important things: to plan and meditate, to think about what really must be done if they are to be successful, to make certain their priorities are in full alignment with the mission of the Church. In managing discretionary time, I have found it useful to assign blocks of time, say ninety minutes, during which I may not be interrupted. I am ruthless in protecting that precious time, instructing my secretary to interrupt me *only* if there is a dire emergency. During that time I try hard to concentrate and focus my efforts.

Nothing that shepherds can do to husband and re-plenish their strength will have as significant an effect as that which relates to the care of their families. President McKay's famous dictum "No other success can compensate for failure in the home" testifies to the importance of keeping the family strong. Wise shepherds understand that without the love, understanding, forbearance, and assistance of their eternal companions, success in the Lord's work would not be forthcoming.

Several years ago, President McKay, in speaking to a group of Church employees, put into perspective what shepherds should concentrate on in their lives. Said he:

> Let me assure you, brethren, that some day you will have a Personal Priesthood Interview with the Savior Himself. If you are interested, I will tell you the order in which He will ask you to account for your earthly responsibilities.
>
> First, He will request an accountability report about your relationship with your wife. Have you actively been engaged in making her happy and ensuring that her needs have been met as an individual?
>
> Second, He will want an accountability report about each of your children individually. He will not attempt to have this for simply a family stewardship report but will request information about your relationship to each and every child.
>
> Third, He will want to know what you personally have done with the talents you were given in the pre-existence.
>
> Fourth, He will want a summary of your activity in your Church assignments. He will not be necessarily interested in what assignments you have had, for in His eyes the home teacher and mission president are probably equals, but He will request a summary of how you have been of service to your fellowmen in your Church assignments.
>
> Fifth, He will have no interest in how you earned

your living, but if you were honest in all your dealings.

Sixth, He will ask for an accountability on what you have done to contribute in a positive manner to your community, state, country, and the world. (Statement given in June 1965, from the notes of Fred A. Baker, a managing director of the Church's Department of Physical Facilities.)

Note that the Lord puts the first emphasis on family, on a priesthood leader's relationships with his spouse and children. He is certainly less interested in how His sons earn a living, though He is most concerned whether they are honest in their dealings.

Whatever else shepherds do, time must be provided for their families. If leaders are as busy and as active as they should be, it will not always be easy to do so. True nobility of character lies in doing what is necessary to build relationships with family members. Efforts to do so require patient perseverence; herein lie the sweetest joys of life.

One of the great tragedies of life is to observe men—and increasingly women—who struggle up the ladder of their careers, perhaps, though not necessarily, over the backs of colleagues, and who, in the process—through carelessness, neglect, or selfishness—lose their families. They divorce their spouses, from whom, in the euphemism of the day, they claim to have "grown apart." Their children drift away, finding no warmth, no giving, no help, no understanding. And then, perhaps in the twilight of their lives, they find that all they've done has turned to ashes. The ladder they climbed was leaning against the wrong wall. It led not to light and joy but to darkness of mind and spirit.

It need not be so. Many there are whose lives are tributes to the happiness that comes from commitments made and renewed daily. President Gordon B. Hinckley tells a sweet and loving story that illustrates the strength and joy

157

that comes from sweet and fulfilling family associations. Said he:

> I think of two friends from my high school and university years. He was a boy from a country town, plain in appearance, without money or apparent promise. He had grown up on a farm, and if he had any quality that was attractive it was the capacity to work. He carried bologna sandwiches in a brown paper bag for his lunch and swept the school floors to pay his tuition. But with all of his rustic appearance, he had a smile and a personality that seemed to sing of goodness. She was a city girl who had come out of a comfortable home. She would not have won a beauty contest, but she was wholesome in her decency and integrity and attractive in her decorum and dress.
>
> Something wonderful took place between them. They fell in love. Some whispered that there were far more promising boys for her, and a gossip or two noted that perhaps other girls might have interested him. But these two laughed and danced and studied together through their school years. They married when people wondered how they could ever earn enough to stay alive. He struggled through his professional school and came out well in his class. She scrimped and saved and worked and prayed. She encouraged and sustained, and when things were really tough, she said quietly, "Somehow we can make it." Buoyed by her faith in him, he kept going through these difficult years. Children came, and together they loved them and nourished them and gave them the security that came of their own love for and loyalty to one another. Now many years have passed. Their children are grown, a lasting credit to them, to the Church, and to the communities in which they live.
>
> I remember seeing them on a plane, as I returned from an assignment. I walked down the aisle in the semidarkness of the cabin and saw a woman, white-haired, her head on her husband's shoulder

as she dozed. His hand was clasped warmly about hers. He was awake and recognized me. She awakened, and we talked. They were returning from a convention where he had delivered a paper before a learned society. He said little about it, but she proudly spoke of the honors accorded him.

I wish that I might have caught with a camera the look on her face as she talked of him. Forty-five years earlier people without understanding had asked what they saw in each other. I thought of that as I returned to my seat on the plane. Their friends of those days saw only a farm boy from the country and a smiling girl with freckles on her nose. But these two found in each other love and loyalty, peace and faith in the future.

There was a flowering in them of something divine, planted there by that Father who is our God. In their school days they had lived worthy of that flowering of love. They had lived with virtue and faith, with appreciation and respect for self and one another. In the years of their difficult professional and economic struggles, they had found their greatest earthly strength in their companionship. Now in mature age, they were finding peace and quiet satisfaction together. Beyond all this, they were assured of an eternity of joyful association through Priesthood covenants long since made and promises long since given in the House of the Lord. (*Ensign*, March 1984, pp. 3–4.)

Shepherds must also take the time for personal self-renewal: reading and pondering the scriptures, praying and meditating, developing talents, participating in hobbies that relax and unburden the soul, and physical exercise. Elder Harold B. Lee had this wise advice concerning meditation: "President McKay sometime ago in talking to the Presidency and the twelve, urged us to give time for more meditation so that we could tune in with spiritual forces that we had a right to and should expect to direct us in our work." (*Conference Report*, October 1962, p. 82.)

In one way, at least, the responsibility to protect and replenish personal strength flows from the broader responsibility the Lord's shepherds have to act as stewards over time, talents, and callings. That responsibility cannot be fulfilled if through misplaced priorities or lack of care they vitiate their strength, undermine their capacities to serve, and "wear away," in Jethro's felicitous words.

# CHAPTER SIX

# In the Shepherd's Footsteps

Each of us walks many paths through life. I grew up on a farm in central Alberta, Canada, never having heard of The Church of Jesus Christ of Latter-day Saints except in the melodramatic novels of Zane Grey. Our farm was twenty-two miles from the nearest town; and in company with all other children in the community, I attended a one-room country school, walking the two miles each way, there and back, every day. How vividly I remember the path to school. It wound through our pastureland and fields, taking the line of least resistance, past the hillside where purple crocuses bloomed in the spring, skirting the slough where wild violets and tiger lilies could be found in June. To the south was a wood where a magpie's hooded nest perched in a tall poplar tree. A ruffed grouse drummed on a log there; and if you were quiet and patient, you could get close enough to watch. Further on were the tumbled rock foundations of a long-abandoned settler's cabin. My brother and I trapped a weasel there one chilly day in October.

Snow came early in that northern land, and each dreary winter's day all I saw along the path to and from school was my elder brother's footsteps in the snow where he had gone ahead to break the trail for me to follow. I carefully placed my feet where he had trod, trying at the same time to keep an eye peeled for signs of a skulking coyote or covey of prairie chickens. But the best part of the trip was my first glimpse of home and the knowledge that soon I would be safe and warm and could bury my face in my mother's apron and feel her loving embrace. Over the years I've walked many paths in many lands, but those magical days of early childhood stay with me. As real as yesterday are the remembered sights and smells and feelings of homecoming on Canada's prairies.

Jesus, too, walked many paths. His teaching and example blazed the trail we each must follow, pointing the way back home to our Father's house. He is "the Shepherd . . . of [our] souls" (see 1 Peter 2:25) and we "the people of his pasture, and the sheep of his hand" (Psalm 95:7). We who are blessed to serve as His undershepherds—as apprentice shepherds, if you will—can learn much from a careful examination of the paths Jesus walked.

From such an examination we learn the essence of leadership in the Lord's kingdom. We learn what He expects of us and how to fulfill our sacred stewardship. Perhaps the most important lesson we learn is that we do not walk the paths of life alone. He is there with us to protect and strengthen, lift and forgive. He promises: "I will go before your face. I will be on your right hand and on your left, and my Spirit shall be in your hearts, and mine angels round about you, to bear you up." (D&C 84:88.)

The paths Jesus walked include the following:

1. *The path of sorrow.* Isaiah spoke of Jesus as "despised and rejected of men; a man of sorrows, and acquainted with grief." (Isaiah 53:3.) Jesus, the triumphant, redeeming Lord, the resurrected, glorified Christ, grieves not for Himself, but in part at least because of the hardness of the hearts of men. Many of God's children "are without affection, and they hate their own blood." (See Moses 7:33.) They refuse to acknowledge Jesus as Savior and Lord and in like manner reject the fatherhood of Elohim. The sad

162

truth is that many live only for this world, denying the "spirit of prophecy and of revelation" (Helaman 4:12), knowing "nothing concerning [God's] mysteries; and then they are taken captive by the devil, and led by his will down to destruction" (Alma 12:11). Is it any wonder that Jesus weeps over our hardness and foolishness? He knows the consequence of that wickedness. "Wherefore should not the heavens weep, seeing these shall suffer?" (Moses 7:37.) Praise be to God for the redeeming sacrifice of Jesus, who "suffered these things for all, that they might not suffer if they would repent; but if they would not repent they must suffer even as [did He]; which suffering caused [Him], even God, the greatest of all, to tremble because of pain, and to bleed at every pore, and to suffer both body and spirit." (D&C 19:16–18.) In His supernal suffering He assumes the burden of our guilt, if we will but repent and come to Him. "In all their affliction he was afflicted, and the angel of his presence saved them: in his love and in his pity he redeemed them; and he bare them, and carried them." (Isaiah 63:9.)

Jesus sorrows at our transitory faith, our seeming inability to put our full trust in God, our incessant demanding to know *why*, our unwillingness to surrender the totality of our heart and will to the Almighty. Faithful Nephi was blessed, as few mortals have been, to hear the words of Elohim, the Father Himself, on this matter: "The words of my Beloved are true and faithful. *He that endureth to the end, the same shall be saved.*" (2 Nephi 31:15; italics added.) Sometimes we have to wait for God's response to our pleas for help or relief.

Jesus sorrows, too, at our spiritual superficiality. He grieves at our unwillingness to struggle to understand the great spiritual truths that bring salvation and exaltation. He weeps when we seek a sign rather than an understanding heart. Our fickleness, our lack of constancy, are an affront to Him. We seem so often unwilling to pay the price to know Him. In one of the greatest sermons of all time, He described Himself as the living bread and water and proclaimed: "Whoso eateth my flesh, and drinketh my blood, hath eternal life; and I will raise him up at the last day. For my flesh is meat indeed, and my blood is drink indeed. He that eateth my flesh, and drinketh my blood, dwelleth in me, and I in him. . . . He that eateth me, . . . shall live by me. This is that bread which came down from heaven: not as your fathers did eat manna, and are dead: he that eateth of this bread shall live for ever." (John 6:54–58.) Many of His listeners, greedy only for the bread of this world, and foolishly seeking a sign of Christ's divinity, murmured, "This is an hard saying; who can hear it?" (John 6:60.) "From that time," John recorded, "many of his disciples went back, and walked no more with him." (John 6:66.)

One can almost sense the sorrow in Jesus' voice when He said to the twelve, "Will ye also go away?" Thank God for the great Peter, who with all of his mortal fallibilities was already deeply committed to Christ. He replied: "Lord, to whom shall we go? thou hast the words of eternal life. And we believe and are sure that thou art that Christ, the Son of the living God." (John 6:67–69.)

Those who are called to serve the Good Shepherd may have to walk the path of suffering with Him. Some in their callings as undershepherds will work with those who are reaping the consequences of sinful actions or experiencing other severe challenges in life. As shepherds strive to help and strengthen their brothers and sisters, their feelings of empathy and sorrow should reflect a Christlike suffering for such tribulations.

Others will be required to walk a more personal path of suffering. Such a one was Polycarp, bishop of Smyrna, a city on the Western coast of Asia Minor. Polycarp was martyred in A.D.156 for his belief in Christ. Unwilling to bow to Caesar and to worship him, the aged bishop was brought into the stadium to be tried by the Roman Proconsul in the presence of a mob of "lawless heathen." Polycarp was ready for his ordeal. He knew he would be martyred, having said to his companions a few days before his arrest, "I must needs be burned alive." As he was entering the stadium there came to Polycarp a voice as it were from heaven: "Be strong, Polycarp, and play the man."

"Curse the Christ," the Proconsul ordered. The reply was simple: "Eighty and six years have I served him, and he hath done me no wrong; how then can I blaspheme my king who saved me?"

The Proconsul persisted: "I have wild beasts; if thou repent not, I will throw thee to them." Boldly Polycarp replied, "Send for them. For repentance from better to worse is not a change permitted to us; but to change from cruelty to righteousness is a noble thing."

Again the Proconsul spoke: "If thou dost despise the wild beasts I will make thee to be consumed by fire, if thou repent not." Courageous Polycarp answered: "Thou threatenest the fire that burns for an hour and in a little while is quenched; for thou knowest not of the fire of the judgement to come, and the fire of the eternal punishment, reserved for the ungodly. But why delayest thou? Bring what thou wilt."

"Polycarp hath confessed himself to be a Christian," proclaimed the Proconsul's messenger to the assembled multitude. "Burn him alive," they raged. Timber and faggots were brought, and Polycarp was submitted to the flames. (See *Martyrium Polycarpi*, a letter from the Church in Smyrna, in *Documents of the Christian Church*, 2nd edition, edited by Henry Bettenson [Oxford University Press, 1986], pp. 9–12.)

Peter, the great apostle, who himself suffered a martyr's death (see John 21:18–19), recognized that divine merit is associated with patient suffering for Christ's sake but that little glory accrues to us if we suffer for our own sins. He wrote: "This is thankworthy, if a man for conscience toward God endure grief, suffering wrongfully. For what glory is it, if, when ye be buffeted for your faults, ye shall take it patiently? but if, when ye do well, and suffer for it, ye take it patiently, this is acceptable with God." (1 Peter 2:19–20.) As we endure undeserved suffering, we develop Christlike attributes that perfect our souls and bring us closer to Him.

2. *The path of loneliness.* Jesus walked the path of loneliness. Who can forget the pathos, the ineffable loneliness in His statement that "the foxes have holes, and the birds of the air have nests; but the Son of man hath not where to lay his head"? (Matthew 8:20.) Jesus knew the pain of false friends: "Have not I chosen you twelve, and one of you is a devil?" (John 6:70.) The human mind cannot understand the terrible loneliness Christ felt on the cross. At that time the Father "seems to have withdrawn the support of His immediate Presence, leaving to the Savior of men the glory of complete victory over the forces of sin and death." (James E. Talmage, *Jesus the Christ* [Salt Lake City: Deseret Book Co., 1983], p. 613.) Only when Jesus understood that His atoning sacrifice had been accepted by the Father and His mission in the flesh was finished did He exclaim, "Father, into thy hands I commend my spirit." (Luke 23:46.) He knows all there is to know about loneliness; we cannot teach *Him* anything, whatever our condition may be.

Daniel Defoe's *Robinson Crusoe,* although published over two and a half centuries ago, has an enduring place in the hearts of every generation of readers. As the sole survivor of a ship caught in a storm and broken apart on a reef near an uninhabited island somewhere off the South American coast, Crusoe had every reason to feel lonely. Washed ashore by the ocean currents, he managed first to survive and then to build a life for himself, using a mixture of materials salvaged from the ship and what was available to him on the island. For a quarter of a century he lived a lonely, solitary life. Then he rescued a young native man from cannibals and civilized him. He called the young man "Friday," after the day of his rescue. After a series of further adventures, Crusoe and Friday left the island, rescued at last.

Crusoe underwent a kind of metamorphosis on the island. At first he was overcome with loneliness and self-pity:

> I had a dismal prospect of my condition, for as I was not cast away upon that island without being driven, as is said, by a violent storm quite out of the course of our intended voyage, and a great way, viz., some hundreds of leagues out of the ordinary course of the trade of mankind, I had great reason to consider it as a determination of Heaven that in this desolate place and in this desolate manner I should end my life; the tears would run plentifully down my face when I made these reflections, and sometimes I would expostulate with myself why Providence should thus completely ruin its creatures and render them so absolutely miserable, so without help abandoned, so entirely depressed that it could hardly be rational to be thankful for such a life. (Daniel Defoe, *Robinson Crusoe* [New York: Bantam Books, 1991], pp. 54–55.)

Later, however, Crusoe found first solace and then deep faith in a study of the Bible, a copy of which he located in a seaman's chest rescued from the wreck. He began to pray, for the first time in his life, and to reflect upon the "distinguishing goodness which had preserved [him]." He

167

began to give thanks to God, "who had so happily and comfortably provided for [him] in [his] desolate condition." Wrote he, "I learned here and again to observe that it is very rare that the providence of God casts us into any condition of life so low, or any misery so great, but we may see something or other to be thankful for, and may see others in worse circumstances than our own." (*Ibid.* p. 240.) Challenges became tests of worthiness for the castaway. Crusoe found he was not alone.

To me that is the great lesson to be learned from Defoe's masterpiece: regardless of what happens to us, we are never alone. When we are torn by despair, crushed by loneliness, when we cry out for a friend, we can turn to Jesus, our ever-present guide and eternal friend. We can talk to Him, and He will understand, for He has felt the same pain, the same sorrow as we feel. "With his stripes we are healed." (Isaiah 53:5.)

3. *The path of temptation.* It may seem difficult at first to understand that Jesus, the very Savior of the world, the Lord God Omnipotent, was tempted, even as we are. Indeed, the temptations of the adversary during Jesus' lonely travail in the wilderness are archetypical of all temptations. Satan attempted to seduce Jesus with appeals to physical appetite, vanity and ego, and the love of power. (See Matthew 4.) Though Satan was vanquished by Jesus' rejection of his diabolical plan, the adversary continued his attempts to lead or seduce Jesus away from His divine mission. Christ's victory in the desert thus was not a final success. His temptations continued throughout His ministry (see Luke 22:28) up to and including the agony of Gethsemane.

As with Jesus, so it is with us. We are not given the opportunity to overcome Satan in a single act of combat. The struggle between flesh and spirit, between God and the devil, is a constant battle throughout life. But, one may ask, was Jesus tempted as I am? In the same way and with the same enticements? After all, He is God, and I am but a weak and fallible mortal. The answer from the scriptures is clear: "We have not an high priest which cannot be touched with the feeling of our infirmities; *but was in all points tempted like as we are, yet without sin.*" (Hebrews 4:15; italics added.)

The Nephite prophets also understood the nature of the temptations of Christ. Alma, speaking of the Savior not yet born into mortality, proclaimed with prophetic clarity, "He shall go forth, suffering pains and afflictions and *temptations of every kind;* and this that the word might be fulfilled which saith he will take upon him the pains and the sicknesses of his people." (Alma 7:11; italics added.) Jesus, then, having been tempted, understands *our* temptations. "In that he himself hath suffered being tempted, he is able to succour them that are tempted." (Hebrews 2:18.) Does He still love us, as soiled and imperfect as we are? Oh, yes! Yes! There is no truth greater than that in all the universe!

One of the temptations the Lord's undershepherds must be particularly wary of is the temptation of power. These prescient words of the Prophet Joseph Smith come to mind. They should be required periodic reading for all undershepherds!

> Behold, there are many called, but few are chosen. And why are they not chosen? Because their hearts are set so much upon the things of this world, and aspire to the honors of men, that they do not learn this one lesson—That the rights of the priesthood are inseparably connected with the powers of heaven, and that the powers of heaven cannot be controlled nor handled only upon the principles of righteousness. That they may be conferred upon us, it is true; but when we undertake to cover our sins, or to gratify our pride, our vain ambition, or to exercise control or dominion or com-

169

pulsion upon the souls of the children of men, in any degree of unrighteousness, behold, the heavens withdraw themselves; the Spirit of the Lord is grieved; and when it is withdrawn, Amen to the priesthood or the authority of that man. Behold, ere he is aware, he is left unto himself, to kick against the pricks, to persecute the saints, and to fight against God. We have learned by sad experience that it is the nature and disposition of almost all men, as soon as they get a little authority, as they suppose, they will immediately begin to exercise unrighteous dominion. (D&C 21:34–39.)

How seductive the lure of power and the prestige that goes with it can be! The acclaim of the people, the virtual adulation in which leaders are held by many members, the hanging-on-every-word attention leaders receive—all are powerful intoxicants, easily capable of corrupting the unwary shepherd. Leaders should, of course, be grateful for the love and support of the Saints. But they must discount personal praise directed at them, recognizing that whatever fraction is deserved rightfully belongs to the Good Shepherd and the Father. We can take little credit if we utilize well gifts and talents that have been bestowed upon us. The credit belongs to the Giver of Gifts, not the receiver. When dealing with the praise of men, perhaps it would be wise to adopt something of the attitude of the Duke of Wellington. "Asked if he were pleased to have been mobbed by the ecstatic population of Brussels on his return from Waterloo [Wellington] rejoined, 'Not in the least; if I had failed, they would have shot me.' " (John Keegan, *The Mask of Command,* p. 163.)

Thomas Cromwell, principal adviser to King Henry VIII of England, is an example of a man of great talent corrupted by power. Cromwell served Henry for ten years (1530–40), during much of which time he occupied all key positions in the English government and exercised complete control

170

over every aspect of its administration. He was always careful, however, to pretend to be acting on the king's authority. Cromwell, an administrative genius, was totally ruthless in the pursuit of his aim to establish the reformation in England and strengthen the power of the king. With a single stroke, he solved the impasse between Henry and the Pope occasioned by the king's wish to divorce Catherine of Aragon and marry Anne Boleyn. Cromwell's solution was elegant in its simplicity: overrule the papacy, remove the Pope from England, and pressure the Archbishop of Canterbury into granting the divorce Henry wanted so desperately. The king had his way; the clergy were browbeaten and bludgeoned into submission; the Archbishop of Canterbury, Thomas Cranmer, appointed by Henry, ruled that the king's marriage to Catherine was void and that his union with Anne was "good and lawful"; the separation from Rome was final.

Henry's foreign wars and extravagant tastes resulted in chronic shortages of government funds. Cromwell saw in the vast treasures held in the monasteries a ready source of money to fill the royal coffers. He presided with an iron hand and ferocious energy over the dissolution of the monasteries, shrinking at nothing to achieve his purpose. By 1540 all monastic institutions — several hundred in all — had ceased to exist, and their property and immense wealth were in the king's hands, to be used according "to the pleasure of Almighty God and to the honour and profit of this realm."

Cromwell's enemies multiplied like vermin. They bided their time, waiting for him to make a mistake. Finally it happened. Cromwell worked and schemed to establish a closer relationship between Henry and the protestant princes of Germany. Central to Cromwell's plan was a marriage alliance between Henry and Anne, the only daughter of the Duke of Cleves, a German nobleman.

Cromwell assured Henry that Anne was unspeakably beautiful. When Henry found she was anything but that, he repudiated Anne and charged Cromwell with deceit and treason. All of Cromwell's numerous and powerful enemies then openly turned against him. He was condemned without trial as a "most false and corrupt traitor" and a "detestable heretic" who had boasted of his power over the king. Taken to the Tower of London, he was kept alive until he had provided the necessary evidence for Henry to obtain a divorce from Anne of Cleves. Cromwell was executed by beheading on July 28, 1540. He died as he had lived, a victim of unbridled ambitions, lack of scruples, and love of power. (For details of Cromwell's life and times see De Lamar Jensen, *Reformation Europe: Age of Reform and Revolution* [Lexington, Mass.: D. C. Heath and Co., 1981], pp. 146–55, and Jasper Ridley, *Henry VIII, the Politics of Tyranny* [New York: Fromm International Publishing Corporation, 1986], pp. 325–44.)

In *Macbeth,* Shakespeare portrays a man in whom the worm of ambition, of greed for power, steadily grows until it leads to his destruction. When told by the three witches (Act I, scene iii) that he will be king hereafter, Macbeth first demurs, insisting he has no ambitions. But the worm begins to grow, and soon Macbeth is plotting murder, vacillating between willingness to kill Duncan the king and momentary shrinking from the dreadful deed. "If it were done, when 'tis done, then 'twere well / It were done quickly," he muses. Then drawing back from the increasingly delicious contemplation of evil, he piously proclaims that Duncan is "here in double trust: / first, as I am his kinsman and his subject, / Strong both against the deed; then, as his host, / who should against his murderer shut the door, / not bear the knife myself." (Act I, scene vii.) Urged on by his avaricious wife ("screw your courage to the sticking-place, / And we'll not fail"), Macbeth succumbs to evil, and the devil leads him thenceforth. Shakespeare's genius portrays the triumph of evil in a man who did not start out bad but ended up with "his secret murders sticking on his hands."

The lesson of the play—that ambition for power and the improper use of power corrupts and ultimately destroys—is universal and applicable in all societies and in every period of history.

Let Jesus be our exemplar in this and all other aspects of our leadership responsibilities. Always meek and humble, He never succumbed to the temptation to abuse power and authority. Humility and meekness are the keys to avoiding the corruption of power. He who fashioned the miracle of the loaves, He who was the Bread of Life, thanked His Father for the bread! On the cross He meekly and submissively finished the work He had been sent to do. Significantly Christ's last words, as He hung on the cross, demonstrated humble obedience: "Father it is finished, thy will is done." (JST Matthew 27:54.)

Some shepherds may be tempted to believe the insidious falsehood that they are indispensable, irreplaceable. Those who feel that way may complain, sulk, or be offended when they are released from whatever responsibility they have been assigned to. They may grumble that their successor isn't up to doing the job properly and even go so far as to withhold their support. Those who act in this way evidently fail to understand that as sure as they are called they will also be released. All that remains to be determined is the timing. It may be sooner or later, but release is inevitable. When the clock is turned on to start their service, it begins the countdown on their release as well. Even those trusted servants who serve for the duration of their mortal lives are released by death from earthly responsibilities. The spirit with which shepherds accept release from a calling is a test of their obedience and humility.

4. *Jesus walked the path of unity.* Jesus and the Father, though separate in person, are one in purpose and in the implementation of their divine mission. That truth is reiterated repeatedly in the scriptures. (See, for example, Matthew 3:17; John 5:19; 10:30, 38; 17:21.) The unity of the Father and Son serves as the example of how the Lord's undershepherds must act. "Be one," the Lord has counseled, "and if ye are not one ye are not mine." (D&C 38:27.) Loyalty to each other, the bearing of each others' burdens, and mutual concern are the hallmarks of faithful shepherds. They know that if the adversary can drive us apart, he will win the day. "We must be knit together in this work as one. . . . We must delight in each other, make others' Conditions our own, rejoice together, mourn together, labor and suffer together . . . as members of the same body." (John Winthrop, "A Model of Christian Charity," in *Issues in American Protestantism: A Documentary History from the Puritans to the Present,* edited by Robert L. Ferm [Garden City, NY: Anchor Books/Doubleday & Co., 1969], p. 10.)

The unity shepherds must feel and practice is not only a practical necessity if the work of the Lord is to be done, but it also arises from a mutual faith in God and in His cause. It is the shared faith that binds us together, each contributing his or her small part toward the accomplishment of our divinely appointed task, each caught up in a cause greater than ourselves.

5. *Jesus walked the path of obedience.* Christ's life provides an eloquent example of His infinite obedience to His Father. He said, "I do always those things that please him." (John 8:29.) Jesus' obedience ransomed us all (Romans 5:8), making possible eternal life for those who, led by the Holy Spirit, become "humble, meek, submissive, patient,

full of love, and all long-suffering" (Alma 13:28). Through obedience we grow spiritually and become more like God. Obedience carries us forward in the Lord's work, even if we do not as yet fully understand the "why" of our service.

How sublime a word is *obedience:* the cornerstone of righteousness, the mark of the true disciple of Christ, the prerequisite for self-mastery, the companion of virtue, the first law of God. Faith and humility are its parents; service and sacrifice, its offspring; celestial joy, its reward.

Faithful shepherds are distinguished by their obedience to God and His prophets. Brigham Young's ministry was marked by humble obedience, by an intense desire and willingness to follow counsel. In early 1840, while leading a group of the Twelve on a mission to England, Brigham penned the following letter to the First Presidency:

> To President Joseph Smith and Counselors:
> Dear Brethren: You no doubt will have the perusal of this letter, and minutes of our conference; this will give you an idea of what we are doing in this country. If you see anything in or about the whole affair, that is not right, I ask, in the name of the Lord Jesus Christ, that you would make known unto us the mind of the Lord, and His will concerning us. I believe that I am as willing to do the will of the Lord, and take counsel of my brethren, and be a servant of the Church, as ever I was in my life; but I can tell you, I would like to be with my old friends; I like new friends, but I cannot part with my old ones for them. (*History of the Church,* 4:119–20.)

Faithful shepherds learn obedience from the holy scriptures and from following the counsel of the living prophets and other Church leaders. They learn obedience by disciplining their lives, by striving always to follow the principles of the gospel, including the laws and ordinances thereof. They learn obedience as the Savior did, by the things they suffer. Their willingness to be obedient is a measure of their love of the Father and the Son. They know that through obedience weak things are made strong. God is bound to reward those who obey Him. (See D&C 82:10.)

Some time ago I spoke to a young man who learned almost too late the role of obedience as the prerequisite for self-mastery. I will call him John, though that is not his real name. He was "born of goodly parents," graduated from Primary, and was active in his priests quorum. Though at that time in his life he attended Church regularly and on the surface was a faithful member, John was already, as a young man, living a double life. He had been introduced to alcohol at a school dance and by the time he graduated from high school was for practical purposes an alcoholic. A year at a large state university only confirmed his appetite for strong drink. His life began to spiral out of control as his grades at university plummeted and his attendance at Church ceased. At the very brink of disaster, John was saved by a loving bishop who said gently, "John, don't you see what you're doing to yourself? Don't you understand where this life-style you've adopted is leading you?" Others, including his parents, had tried to talk to John previously, but he had pushed them away, unwilling to listen, unable to admit he was in trouble. But something in the bishop's voice and manner touched John's heart. "I went to my room that night," he recounted, "and for the first time in my life I prayed. Oh I had gone through the motions lots of times previously—I'd mumbled a few trite phrases, anxious to get it all over with. But this time, I *really* prayed, asking God to help me because I just couldn't do it myself. There came to me a sudden realization that in debasing myself I also, in a sense, crucified Christ afresh. It was almost more than I could bear.

For the first time ever I pled for forgiveness and pledged obedience to the Father's will."

From that moment on, John's life began to change. He stopped drinking, began to come back to Church, read the scriptures daily, and prayed fervently for strength and forgiveness. Obedience replaced rebellion as he tasted the sweet fruits of repentance. His "drinking buddies" soon abandoned him, but he no longer cared. He had found clean and wholesome friends at Church and, above all else, a Special Friend, who knew and understood him. He had found joy in walking the paths Jesus had trod so long ago.

Yes, Jesus walked many paths, and so must we. "Come follow me," He says. As we follow in His footsteps, our lives will change. We will become more effective and obedient servants, better human beings, more like the Good Shepherd in whose cause we labor.

# Index